Australasian Catholic Coalition for Church Reform

The Australasian Catholic Coalition for Church Reform (ACCCR) was established in 2011; it comprises a network of 19 member organisations across Australia and New Zealand. Member groups are committed to the Catholic faith and foster collaboration and support in seeking renewal of our Church. The Coalition disseminates messages of hope and opportunity for a Church that models the teachings of Jesus. It is guided by Vatican II and the leadership of Pope Francis with a strong commitment to co-responsibility for the Church's mission among all Catholics. The voice of the people must be heard and attended to at all levels in the Church, with synodality ensuring the equality of all, especially women.

ACCCR is particularly concerned that the institutional Church does not yet embody the vision of Vatican II for a truly collegial Church in which decisions respect local cultures, communities and circumstances. Rather, it too often appears to be focussed on centralism, legalism, and control with few effective structures for listening and dialogue, and often more concerned with its institutional image and interests than the spirit of Christ.

ACCCR seeks a Church whose leadership and role in the world reflect the teachings of Jesus and model the best of Christian values, a Church which is accountable, transparent and inclusive in its decision-making reflecting the sense of the faith of the people. We seek a model of Church that Jesus expects from us in this millennium, requiring uncommon courage, a commitment to changes in how we do and are church, and openness to radical conversion, reform and renewal.

Contents

The Australian Plenary: An Agenda for Reform?

The Australian Plenary Council is part of a global movement of reform and renewal longed for by Catholics across the world. The Plenary Council has been called in response to the findings of the Royal Commission into Institutional Responses to Child Sexual Abuse and other challenges and failings; it is an opportunity for significant renewal in the Church in Australia.

As a voice for lay Catholics, the Australasian Catholic Coalition for Church Reform (ACCCR) convened a series of Convocations in 2021 to promote the Plenary Council and support its task of renewing the Church in Australia. We are all journeying together to the Council and beyond.

In May 2021, the first Convocation of Australian Catholics, conducted during the COVID pandemic, using *Zoom* technology, featured Sr Joan Chittister OSB. It attracted many thousands who seek change in our Church. Joan called for lay Catholics to be treated 'as equals, as seekers, as spiritual adults. Old styles of worship, old criteria of piety, old ways of relating to the world – good as all of them may once have been – cannot build for us a new Jerusalem in this place in this time... when the forces of history face us with new challenges'. Joan asserted prophetically that Catholicism must grow up, 'beyond the parochial to the global, beyond one system and one tradition, to a broader way of looking at life and its moral, spiritual, ethical frameworks.'

The second Convocation, in August, was opened by Dr Miriam Rose Ungunmerr Baumann, the 2021 Senior Australian of the Year,

and addressed by other prominent and thoughtful Catholic leaders: Debra Zanella, Dr Jessie Rogers and Robert Fitzgerald with a concluding summary by Professor Emeritus John Warhurst. With a tighter focus on the Plenary Council as we drew nearer to the first session in October, they addressed issues related to deepening connections with Aboriginal and Torres Strait Islander traditions; the Plenary Council in its international context; hearing the voice of the people in the Church; and inclusion, particularly ensuring the equality of women, inclusion of marginalised groups, synodality and governance.

When the agenda for the Plenary Council was published in June this year, it was greeted with widespread dismay and disappointment among Catholics hoping for a serious examination and analysis of the weighty challenges confronting us. We were given a set of unnecessarily general, and sometimes superficial, questions on how we might respond to a broad, unspecified call to action. The questions also lack context and neglect the parlous state of the Church in Australia. Some are stuck in the general discussion of three years ago and appear not to consider the 17,500 submissions. To address these deficiencies, after extensive consultation with its 19 member groups and informed by the public submissions to the Plenary Council process, ACCCR has included a considered response to the agenda questions as the last chapter.

This booklet contains the views of prominent and thoughtful Catholics on the challenges facing the Plenary Council and the

Coalition's response to the agenda proposing necessary changes in our Church.

We now call on Plenary Council members to respond to Pope Francis' hopes for a new era of synodality where we will all walk together, listening to a range of voices. This is the model of Church that Jesus expects from us in this millennium; it will require uncommon courage and a commitment to changes in how we do and are church. For this to happen, we must be open to radical conversion, reform and renewal.

Australasian Catholic Coalition for Church Reform, comprising

Australian Reforming Catholics

Be the Change Aotearoa (NZ)

Cardijn Community Australia

Catholics For Renewal

Catholics Speak Out

Communities of the Way (WA)

Concerned Catholics Canberra Goulburn

Concerned Catholics Tasmania

Concerned Catholics Wagga Wagga

Concerned Catholics Wollongong

Cyber Christian Community (WA)

For the Innocents

Inclusive Catholics

Rainbow Catholics InterAgency for Mission

SA Catholics for an Evolving Church

Toowoomba Catholics for Church Reform

VOCAL (Voices of Catholic Australian Laity)

WATAC (Women and the Australian Church)

WWITCH (Women's Wisdom in the Church)

The Spiritual Mountains of the New Millennium

Joan Chittister, OSB

Joan Chittister is one of the most influential religious and social leaders of our time. For 50 years she has passionately advocated on behalf of peace, human rights, women's issues, and church renewal. A much sought-after speaker, counselor, and clear voice that bridges across all religions, she is also a best-selling author of more than 60 books, hundreds of articles, and an online column for the National Catholic Reporter (USA). Joan has received numerous writing awards and honours for her work, and is a noted international lecturer.

Any reflection on contemporary spiritual life in an era of global issues, ecumenical perspectives and theological development must be made from two perspectives: one social, the other biblical.

Socially, the population of the earth is about 8 billion people. Almost half of them live in Asia. Two-thirds of those live in either of two countries – China and India.

The world's literacy rate has risen 20% from 66% in 1979 to 86% in 2021. The world is growing, is developing, and is **not Catholic**.

In 1950, less than 30%, one third of the world, lived in cities. Since 2018 over 55% – more than half of them – do.

And all of that means what? It means that religion is not regional anymore. It means that racial colours are not regional anymore. Language is not regional anymore. And, most of all, it means that God speaks in many tongues – not just ours.

It also means that Catholicism must grow up, that things are changing beyond the parochial to the global, beyond one system and one tradition, to a broader way of looking at life and its moral, spiritual, ethical, and social frameworks.

In a global village, respect for all creation is basic and understanding is its key.

As a result, in a world such as this, religion must be about more than documents and doctrines, about rules and religious conventions in a very unconventional world where ecumenism and unity are warring– and at the very same time.

The second perspective out of which I fashion these reflections, then, is a spiritual one. Two spiritual insights challenge contemporary spirituality today.

The first is a Hasidic tale about a disciple who was puzzled by the scripture passage that says that 'children of Israel at the foot of Mount Sinai stood afar off from it.'

'Why would they do that?' the disciple asked.

And the Rabbi said, 'The children of Israel stood at a distance from Sinai because they knew that miracles are for those who have little faith! And so, in good heart, they avoided them.'

The lesson is clear: the image of Israelites refusing to approach Sinai and its wonders reminds us not to rely on divine interventions to save us from a changing world.

We must work those miracles ourselves.

The real problem is that what we do depends on what we are inside ourselves, because it is what's in us driving us on that is the real value in what we are.

Secondly, when our own scriptures teach us 'do this in memory of me' over and over again, we must begin to realise that past actions are really past. It is the present that must be continually freshened, stretched, fulfilled now, renewed and reformed now.

What we as a holy people did in ages before this one to scratch out of thick forests and vast lands a missionary church is over now. What it meant to establish a Christian presence in a new world that was antagonistic to it, marks us still.

What it took to maintain the faith, to recognise individual rights, to accept as determinative the prisms of difference in the midst of a pluralistic world, tried and tested the humanity of humanity.

What it cost to accept freedom of conscience in a world where states under papal rule, the peace of Augsberg, theocratic theology and wars of religion were long gone and well dead – is for all intents and purposes now basically accomplished.

It is today that God waits for us to come to grips with what it really means to be 'the Christian community' now.

No, we are not in transition to a new form of spirituality because we failed in the past. We are in transition to a new form of spiritual life precisely because we succeeded in the past. We succeeded in creating entire Church school systems and Catholic education became mainstream. That was a miracle.

We succeeded in building systems that absorbed immigrants and now we are a pluralistic culture in a pluralistic world. That was a miracle.

Now we must find new meaning, new purpose, new vision, new miracles in a world totally mainstream but changing everywhere now. The deeply spiritual life – not simply pious practices; the challenges of faith – not simply the comforts of ritual; the needs of the present – not

simply our past achievements are the only things that can make the spiritual life truly spiritual again.

We stand on the brink of a millennium that has never known so much violence, and most of all, inhuman inequality.

We need more, now and here, than Christianity warmed over. We need to do more than go to church. We need to work miracles of our own. Why? Anything else is an attempt to pass off as viable the responses of the past rather than accept as scripture the present will of God for us – as equals, as seekers, as spiritual adults, as both men and women in a church that men think they own. Old styles of worship, old criteria of piety, old ways of relating to the world – good as all of them may once have been – cannot build for us a new Jerusalem in this place at this time.

The forces of history face us with new challenges. New visions of equality and community are calling us in this day. The priesthood of the people is a priesthood dearly to be sought if the Church is ever to be church, is ever to be whole. But how? 'If you wish to see the valleys,' the mystic Kahlil Gilbran wrote 'climb to the mountain top'. Which means what?

The spiritual life now, as the spiritual life has always been, is about being taken up mountains by the God who leads us always beyond ourselves.

Ancient Greek, Hebrew, Roman and Asian religious mythos, all considered mountains the nearest places on earth to heaven.

Mountains, the teachings claimed, the points where earth touched heaven, were places where the human could touch the divine. Mountains were places where people could contact God!

It is understandable then that there are eight mountains in Israel's history of life with God where the people are brought

to stark challenge and so to new growth: Sinai, Gilboa, Olivet, Moriah, Carmel, Hermon, Gerizim and the Mount of the Beatitudes.

It is these mountains which yet today, I believe, challenge us, too. A few of them we climb with daily devotion; some of them, I believe, we have yet to scale if the spiritual life – if religion/the Church – is to be the catalyst, the prophetic voice in this time that it once was in the past.

Mount Sinai

First, Israel's greatest mountain was Mount Sinai.

It was on Sinai, remember, that God flamed in the burning bush and said to Moses, 'Moses, come no further... stay where you are for where you are is holy ground.'

It was on Sinai that Yahweh gave the law that would lead Israel beyond narcissism, beyond its own headstrong ambitions to become its best and truest self.

Sinai is the mountain of spiritual development. What is learned and taught here determines personal development – development that can change the world. It is the mountain Christians know well. For long years, our approach to Sinai – to the will of God – teetered between God's goodness and our concentration on sin – on spiritual control. And so a spirituality centered in negation that discolours sex and gender tended to eclipse the learnings of life around us, yes, but not only.

The mountain of spiritual development also told us that there was a great deal more to life than negation, than 'don't', than fear. There was the love of God and the presence of God everywhere, the call of God to the universal goodness of all races and nations, and the goodness of God for each of us to taste ourselves.

The mountain of spirituality that centred us on the will of God for all was also the mountain that promised us salvation – which too often we explored with too rigid an intensity.

But thanks to Vatican II we know faith-sharing now as well as the discipline of private prayer and public rituals. We know scripture study, we read it ourselves. We know liturgical theology. We know that the spiritual life – the Jesus story – is the gospel trumpet to goodness for which no catechism, no Sunday school attendance record substitutes. We are even learning now that we drown from the lack of soul that plagues us when we substitute religion for spirituality.

Then we are nothing more than religious copies of the real thing – cultists who join together for no totally compelling reason except, perhaps, for social acceptance or spiritual security.

Sinai – the mountain of spiritual development, of spiritual growth, of spiritual commitment – is where our spiritual development is meant to develop.

It is what keeps our eye on the beckoning footsteps of God to new life, new law.

> *For over 50 years now, we have been trying to scale this mountain of renewal together: lay/clerical, women/men, religious/secular.*

Mount Gilboa

The second mountain of spirituality is Mount Gilboa where Saul dies, of whom scripture says, 'God regretted having made Saul king,' and so made way for David and new life. On Gilboa, the old world fades from view and turns from one vision to another: from Saul's vengeful rigor to David's delight in life.

Gilboa is the Mountain of letting go.

For almost 50 years now we have been scaling the mountain of Church renewal/reform. We have been about taking down the barriers of clericalism: opening the altar rails that kept the faithful consumers rather than celebrants of Eucharist. We've been translating the ancient foreign language that distanced the Incarnation and kept the clear presence of God in life behind a Plexiglas of mystery and misunderstanding, magic, formalism, and fear.

For over 50 years now, we have been trying to scale this mountain of renewal together: lay/clerical, women/men, religious/secular.

We have been trying to re-evaluate every phase of Church life, re-examine every liturgical service for inclusion, redefine every theological explanation given for the way women are 'churched' but not men, for instance. We have restructured every organisational jot and tittle of our parish lives: deacons, parish administrators, liturgists, servers and Eucharistic ministers.

But, too often, we have been ignored and repulsed until more and more faithful have left the pews and the clerical politics of it all to rediscover our God in other places and new and welcoming ways. The laity have found God in the sacramental dimensions of life as well as the crucibles of sacrifice, suffering and pain, and through it all found a God who is more sweet–merciful, loving, accepting and healing–than sour.

So we have brought ourselves beyond rigidity, like David, to delight in new ways of seeing new things, and new ways of seeing old things as well. We have begun intentional communities, book clubs, and the most dangerous group in the Church: women's book clubs! We have discovered that organs are no closer to God than guitars, drums, trumpets; that boys are no more capable of carrying water and wine than girls are; that women, too, can read

and that the fast days of life are no holier than the feast days of life – not by one ounce.

We have let go of one kind of spirituality – a dependent, immature, military, and childish one – one in which we were doomed to failure. We have learned to go to God with harp and dance, like David, awash and aware and in praise of delight after delight after delight of celebration vs. clericalism.

Mount Gilboa is the mountain of the delight in letting go of rigidity without which a spiritual life that nurses or thrives on negation can ever come to maturity. Yet we face there, still, a mentality of hierarchy and secular unworthiness that stand in stolid separation of the clerical from the baptised, of men from women.

But in the end it is Gilboa, letting go of the past, that will determine the future of the Church, that will decide whether the Church of Vatican II will be allowed to grow or become this generation's new 'Old Catholic Church.'

Mount Olivet

The third mountain challenging us today is Mount Olivet. On Mount Olivet, with the crucifixion of Jesus, Israel finds itself faced with a choice between old temples and dimmed prophecies about a suffering servant and a meek messiah.

Clearly, Mount Olivet is the mountain of solidarity with the poor and oppressed.

The spiritual life has for long claimed its beginnings at the foot of the cross, in the slums of the world, with the forgotten of humankind; wherever, in whomever the Christ was being crucified now; at the bottom of the bottom.

And today we see it yet. There are both ministers and laity, religious congregations and diocesan officials, in soup kitchens and shelters, in hospitality centres and courts, in television and media, in research and law, in mobile clinics in shanty towns and giving literacy lessons under lean-to shelters, in militarised borders and in bad neighbourhoods where 'nice' people do not go.

We see the laity being Church, beyond ritual and rubric.

The Church that created the Catholic school system, and the hospital system, now creates low-income housing, tutors for poor children, hospitality centres and daycare programs. We are each there to be a voice where the voices of the poor are never heard. Unfortunately, the leaders of this vibrant Church say little themselves.

Heavy yet, with the ministries of the previously poor, churches and religious communities are all struggling to climb Mount Olivet again in a world where Church schools in the inner city have more neighbourhood Protestant kids and fewer parish children every day. So, too often, the Church leaves there. Now a once immigrant Church has become a suburban Church while new immigrants everywhere are hungry, voiceless, churchless and alone.

In a world where women are the poorest of the poor we tell single mothers that they have got to get a job because parishes do not provide child care to enable it. And then the same men tell the same women that the problem with this country is that we have working mothers.

Indeed Mount Olivet is the mountain that reminds us for whom we really exist – the hungry, the imprisoned, the homeless, the unemployed – and keeps the eye of our souls on the oppressed.

Sinai – godliness – the search for the will of God; Gilboa – renewal;

Our young are more distant from the Church and religion than they have been since our beginnings

and Olivet – identification with the poor, are mountains we have climbed with a degree of alacrity. But there are other mountains up which God is leading us if we want to be spiritual people now, and only faith can persuade us to continue the journey.

Mount Moriah

On Mount Moriah, for instance, Abraham was called to sacrifice Isaac, his everything, his future and his past. It was a chilling moment for him, we know, because it is a chilling moment for us, too.

Just when things seem to be at their worst for us, just when ministers are scarce and resources are slim, just when our young are more distant from the Church and religion than they have been since our beginnings, just when attendance is low and tensions are high over the very issues that the Church has always seemed most united about, we are called to sacrifice our past certainties about marriage, divorce, sexuality, other religions, and clerical-episcopal authority. It is a tense time while many are now holding onto one world because they are fearful of the other.

Just when our energy is failing, our churches are closing, and our old age knows no heir, we are asked, like Abraham, on Mount Moriah, to begin again, to sacrifice again.

Mount Moriah is the mountain of sacrifice. At one level we have already climbed it. We are, after all, still here, you and I, in this half new, half old Church. You and I are still braving questions we never thought we'd ask, like: why not women deacons, why not

lay boards that are really boards rather than clerical cheer leaders, why not synods with lay delegates chosen by lay people, why not married priests, women priests, even women cardinals?

Indeed, here we are, still following in the dark, still hoping to find the ram in the bush, the way out of the ennui and despair the excommunications and defections, the gauntlets and the standoffs, the unending Christian legalism, the place where answers are aplenty but crucial questions are being disallowed.

It is a climb full of doubt and full of reservations. We give ourselves to these new things, but not entirely and not without caution and definitely not without hearing about 'good sense' and the 'good business practices' Judas taught us.

The poor sleep in the streets while we rent out empty parish houses or tax parishes to maintain empty seminaries. Inner-city gangs run the street while we close schools no longer Catholic enough to keep open.

We fight for the rights of the unborn but too often fail to be as invested in the needs of the born but illiterate, the born but unwanted, the born but underfed.

We have learned, as Church people it seems, to compute our pension plans; we have learned as Church people to invest our retirement funds; we have learned as Church people to provide for ourselves very well.

We have even learned to 'cost out' our facilities and ministries with professional precision: so much per foot for this auditorium, so much per hour for this break-out room. So much per chord for this organist.

There's nothing wrong, of course with being realistic about expenses but when; 'costing out' becomes a euphemism for lack of sacrifice, lack of largesse, lack of Christianity, then, perhaps, we need to remember our history and realise again that the lavishness with which we as a church deal with others is the lavishness with which God will deal with us as a church.

We are called to Mount Moriah, the mountain of sacrifice. Mount Moriah is where we must go, as church, to spend ourselves to the end. Church is not a place where people come anymore, that ended with Vatican II. Church is the people to whom we all must go.

The old Church is not dying. The old Church with its parochial provincialism is long dead. The only question for us now is what do we want to be caught dead doing as we change: renewal, revival, or recommitment to a resurrected church?

It is time for a new spirituality of sacrifice.

There is a difference between choosing the things of Yahweh and the things of religion.

Mount Carmel

Mount Carmel is the mountain of choice. On Mount Carmel, Elijah challenged the people to choose between true gods and false gods, between what was really important in the spiritual life and what was simply standard brand piety.

We find ourselves faced with deciding between what is really important and what is not between the novenas, the rosaries, maybe even between the Sunday mass and personal efforts to end sexism or racism, to leave behind the life-building gifts of justice or equality. The problem is that there is a difference between choosing the things of Yahweh and the things of religion.

Indeed, in this time it is we who are being called to choose again.

We are being forced to make decisions about the role of the

Church, the stuff of sanctity, the nature of spirituality, all over again. What is really needed now? What should we really be doing now? What people really have claim on the gospel now, on us now? It's time to reconsider.

It is no longer enough to do church and call that the spiritual life.

It is no longer enough to do theology and call that the spiritual life.

It is no longer enough even simply to do 'good' right now and call that the spiritual life.

Now, we must do the gospel again. We must face the hard new questions of this age in new ways.

Is it really holy to deny two pronouns for the human race and say absolutely nothing about the physical-intellectual equality of women as human beings?

Is it really Christian to support nuclear weaponry which threatens all life, while at the same time condemn to hell a poor woman who refuses a child because she can't feed it?

Is it truly spiritual to say not a word about gun control and then decry street violence?

Clearly, it is one thing to send chaplains to bedsides; it is another thing to advocate for medical insurance.

The point is that choice is a tool of sanctity. Mount Carmel is the mountain that calls us to choose again between the commonplace and the charismatic, between piety and sanctity, between religion and spirituality.

Mount Hermon

Mount Hermon, easily the highest mountain in Israel, has always been seen as a sacred mountain. It is not surprising, then, that it is on Mount Hermon that Jesus becomes transfigured.

But Jesus does not reveal himself to the apostles with Nathan the

What have you questioned in the Church lately and who knows it?

priest or David the king – not with the leaders of either the state or the synagogue. No, Jesus reveals himself to the apostles with Moses and Elijah, the prophets!

Jesus appears with Moses, the liberator, and with Elijah, the prophet, whom King Ahab called 'that troublemaker of Israel'.

Mount Hermon is the sterling call to the people of God to also be a prophetic voice in a world far too silent while global warming and land mine treaties, climate change treaties, nuclear treaties, are being ignored, and civil rights legislation is being eroded away while laser weapons go on being developed in peacetime!

The question from Mount Hermon to those who call ourselves spiritual is, 'What have you questioned in the Church lately and who knows it?' For whom have you and your parishes, your prayer groups and faculties, your communities and congregations, spoken lately and who knows it? For what have you and the Church as a Christian community stood for lately – daycare, immigrants on an island, and who knows it?

Once our churches as churches had a prophetic presence in society, we hid the slaves. We supported the labour movement. We adopted foreign missions. We opened Church-affiliated schools. We integrated parishes. And everybody knew it and nobody called it political.

Now we have multiple individuals, a committee here and there, being prophetic signs in closed societies. But we give little sign, if any, that the parishes themselves even notice, or churches even care about the great needs, the deep hurts in society.

We quarrel over civil rights for the LGBTQI community and then call such immorality moral.

We deplore support for the poor and call it welfare and clamour f or welfare for the rich and call it tax reform.

We turn penniless and frightened immigrants away from our gates and call it national defence.

But a prophetic Church, a spiritual people, cares only for the needs of the poor, the outcast, the powerless, who wait for us to speak for them with pleading hearts.

Possessed by the demons of depression but still begging for crumbs, they wait full of hope at the bottom of Mount Hermon again today.

Big buildings and new churches – architectural leftovers from past prophetic impulses – will not save an institution that fails to use its corporate power to confront the corporate powers of the world because the benefactors won't like it or the bishop doesn't want publicity or the pastor won't approve or, worse, because the parishioners themselves will be upset by it.

If we settle down, in the name of spirituality, and become establishment people, our establishment shall fall like all the temples before us.

Mount Hermon is the mountain that calls us to prophetic presence.

Mount Gerizim

Mount Gerizim, the mount of Samaria, is the mount of equality at which Jesus called a foreign woman six times divorced to be an evangelist in his name.

Since only men had the right to divorce, we are clearly meant to realise that the woman has been six times abandoned, not six times fickle!

But Jesus calls us here in shocking terms to face the challenge feminism brings to a spirituality patriarchal in origin, to a society hierarchical in structure and to a world so single-sexed in vision that it sees with only one eye, hears with only one ear, and thinks with only one-half of the human brain – and it shows! But Jesus surrounded himself with women and sent them out as disciples everywhere. There is no doubt about the call. The Church is segregated – the Church needs to be integrated!

The fact is that a world that rapes its rainforests, pollutes its rivers, beats, enslaves, underpays and suppresses its women – a world that now threatens the very existence of the planet in the name of 'defence' – needs a new world view, needs the presence of the other half of the human race, needs the rest of the human agenda brought to the council tables, the synods, the seminaries, the sacristies of the world, if the human race is ever to be fully human.

'If only you would recognise the gift that has been given you,' Jesus says to the woman, 'you would ask me to give you water.' Listen carefully: you can hear the implication clearly – You would… quit waiting for someone else to give you the right to be the fullness of yourself.

Or to put it more directly: Stand up! Speak out!

Until women and men climb Mount Gerizim together – women teaching, men listening to women as Jesus does here – the will of God is yet to be fulfilled. This call of women to the Woman at the Well as evangelists is, of course, true, real, authentic, but hopelessly incomplete.

How is it that in the face of the woman at the well anyone can exclude women from the centre of the human race, from the centre of the church, in the name of God? How is it that we can castigate people who have the sense to ask these questions and call ourselves spiritual at all?

The notion that any psychologically/spiritually healthy human being – either man or woman, female or male – will join in great numbers an organisation that is blatantly sexist, is a psychedelic dream.

Mount Gerizim is the mountain of the feminine dimension of the spiritual life.

Mount of the Beatitudes

Finally, we, like Israel, find ourselves confronted today with the Mount of the Beatitudes where no one is excluded from responsibility for the Christian life.

The Mount of Beatitudes is the mountain of inclusiveness and the blessing of peacemakers, of the pure of heart, of the poor in spirit, of the merciful, the meek, the mourning, of those who hunger and thirst for righteousness and those who are willing to be persecuted for righteousness.

I think these are the mountains of the spiritual life which, to find God, must be scaled today, I think, if spirituality is to survive, thrive, endure and explode in the twenty-first century.

1. Sinai – the mountain of personal spiritual development.

2. Gilboa – the mountain of letting go of yesterday's Church.

3. Olivet – the mountain of solidarity with the poor.

4. Moriah – the mountain of sacrifice for sake of others.

5. Carmel – the mountain of holy choice.

6. Hermon – the mountain of prophetic presence.

7. Gerizim – the mountain of feminine equality.

and finally, the most ordinary of them all,

8. The Mount of the Beatitudes with its unlimited inclusiveness.

The mountains are clear:

- to be spiritual people in the century to come we must be holy people, not just church-going people;

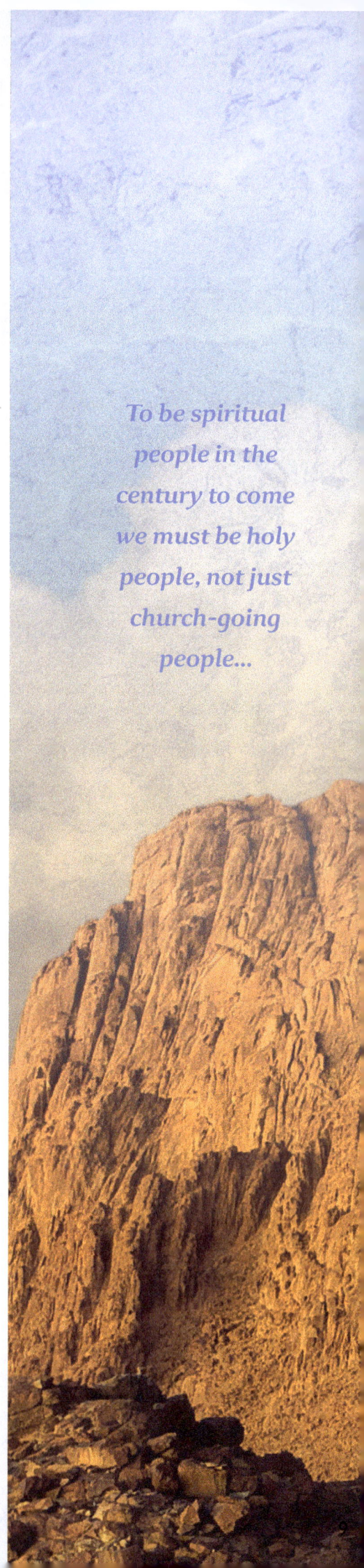

- we must be free people, not just rule-keeping people;

- we must be people passionately involved on behalf of the poor, not just generous people;

- we must be theologically discriminating people, not just docile people;

- we must be prophetic people, not just patiently passive people;

- we must be feminist people, not dualistic, hierarchical, patriarchal people.

We must be people who recognise that it is not that we are the Church that is important. What is important is that we remember that we are what is left of the gospel in this changing time.

Israel was called to be mountain-climbing people. And so are we.

We are called to keep our hearts on Sinai, to rely on faith, not miracles; to foster in this next millennium not simply the spirituality of church-going but the spirituality of the prophetic heart.

And that means what?

The story tells us of a prophet who ran through the streets night after night waving a flaming torch. 'Prophet,' the people cried, 'where are you going with that torch?'

'I'm going to burn the temple down,' the prophet cried.

'But why would you ever do a thing like that?' the people shouted.

'So you remember,' the prophet shouted as she ran, 'to pay less attention to the trappings of the temple and more attention to the will of God.'

The philosopher Boethius reminds us that, 'Every age that is dying is a new one coming to life.'

You are carriers of this new age. What you are, the world will be. Don't give the world private pietism in the name of spirituality; don't give the world the trappings of religion – give us life!

For discussion:

1. Joan states that 'Catholicism must grow up'. What does this mean to you?

2. How can the Australian Plenary Council help us to 'scale this mountain of renewal together: lay/clerical, women/men, religious/secular'?

3. How can we 'pay less attention to the trappings of the temple and more attention to the will of God'.

To be spiritual people in the century to come we must be holy people, not just church-going people...

Women in the Church – Inclusion and Equality

Debra Zanella

Debra Zanella is the Chief Executive Officer of Ruah Community Services in Western Australia. Debra has 20 years' experience in the community sector and is a strong advocate for vulnerable and disadvantaged people. She is inspired by the prophetic views of Joan Chittister and shares her concern for the unequal treatment of women in the Catholic Church, a topic not raised in Plenary Council 'agenda questions'.

Growing up I recall my Mother saying that time passes more quickly the older you get. To a young child, time is something that is beyond comprehending; a week feels like forever and a year as something that will never come. As I age, I have become more conscious of the passage of time as a river that sweeps me along my own life journey. I think about TS Eliot's line in the *Four Quartets*, that life is one of ceaseless exploration that at the end of this exploration finds as at the place we started.

> *We shall not cease from exploration*
> *And the end of all our exploring*
> *Will be to arrive where we started*
> *And know the place for the first time..*

Eliot reminds us in his poem that life – something that we in our postmodern society forget – is not something to achieve, to grasp as a final prize, but a never-ending process of exploring and arriving. It is not 'Groundhog Day', but an exploring and arriving that brings us deeper into a new awareness of who we are until the last of our days. Eliot is a reminder to me that this ceaseless exploration means that knowing is always partial, always unfolding, and it requires the traveller to be open, to come without judgement and assumptions to that which will be discovered.

May E Hunt suggests the same when she says that *'All theology is partial, limited and contextual... that everyone can do theology insofar as we seek to ask and answer questions of ultimate meaning and value.'* Eliot and Hunt are my starting point and reminder as I give attention to the question of 'what success at the Plenary Council would look like'. I share my reflections here on success, given where we are at in our collective history and my own experience as a woman, a leader in the social services sector working with vulnerability and disadvantage, and as a white privileged woman within the Catholic tradition. I also acknowledge that I bring many assumptions and judgements to this process, noting that my hope for a successful Plenary Council would be that it:

1. Has a commitment to becoming a new Catholic Church that as WATAC in Australia Women Preach proclaims that we intend to model the Church we want to be – inclusive, diverse, and welcoming;

2. Is a church that holds up a new looking glass – one that is not based on a patriarchal normative experience –through which to see, hear and discern the movement of the Spirit in our time.

3. Embraces a New Theology – that our theological reflections are indelibly shaped by our human, bodily experiences, and in particular the bodily experiences of women.

In the following passages I have attempted to express these three hopes a little more fully.

A New Catholic Church

I start the answer to what would Plenary Council success be for me as a woman, and as a Catholic woman, with the words of James Carroll in *Toward a New Catholic Church: The Promise of Reform* when he says:

'It is too soon to know the answer to these (this) questions. But to put my own conviction plainly: the twenty-first century desperately needs an intellectually vital, ecumenically open, and morally sound Catholicism, a Catholicism fully itself – that is, a Catholicism profoundly reformed. The world needs a new Catholic Church.'

> *...the lens through which we see, understand and give meaning to the experience of women, of LGBTQI people, of First Nations people.*

Carroll, a prophetic voice calling for the need for a Vatican III, describes clearly that the delivery of such a new Catholic Church requires the deconstruction of the underlying structures, beliefs and systems that feed the current injustices. In writing about institutional and clerical abuse he says:

Here is the lesson: a power structure that is accountable only to itself will always end by abusing the powerless. Even then, it will paternalistically ask to be trusted to repair the damage. Never again. Not only the discredited bishops who protected abusive priests must go; the whole system that produced them must go. Full democratic reform is the Catholic Church's only hope. If

we can take the Body of Christ in hand, we can take the Church in hand too.

- A church that is inclusive, diverse, and welcoming requires the total reformation of the structures that have prevented it from being such a church. You cannot tinker around the edges with small reforms that provide the appearance of change but do nothing to change the underlying structures which have harmed and continue to harm and exclude the faithful. Beliefs around the role of women, systems and structures that perpetuate patriarchy and the centralising of power, teachings and actions that refuse the full expression of a person's God given humanity must change. There can be no equivocation, no half measures. They must be dismantled. The wall of Jericho must fall. Nothing less than this is required.

A New Looking Glass

To have a new Catholic Church, as I have suggested in the passage above, requires a new looking glass. A looking glass, as described in Lewis Caroll's *Alice in Wonderland* provides a perspective that challenges the normative experience. It offers a view that is different to what is currently offered. It is a view that challenges the dominance of patriarchy as the social context for the Old and New Testament, a dominance which has passed over the experience of women, their lives, and their bodies. This context, despite the thousands of years that have passed, continues to be held as the lens through which we see, understand, and give meaning to the experience of women, of LGBTQI people, of First Nations people. The lens of patriarchy continues to be the normative lens through which the

Catholic Church looks and thus informs its decisions and actions. Mary Hunt in her work *Fierce Tenderness*, cites that wonderful passage from Rosemary Radford Ruther writing on the impact of the patriarchal normative views when she says:

Whatever denies, diminishes, or distorts the full humanity of women, is, therefore, appraised as not redemptive. Theologically speaking whatever diminishes or denies the full humanity of women must be presumed not to reflect the divine or an authentic relation to the divine, or to reflect the authentic nature of things, ought to be the message or work of an authentic Redeemer or a community of redemption.

Whilst I do not purport to be a theologian, the challenge that Reuther's work presents is that if we accept patriarchy, consciously or unconsciously, as the normative assumption behind the Old and New Testament, then diminishment of the Divine occurs. That is, the full aspect of the Divine cannot come into being. The acceptance and valuing of the human person in all its arrays is necessary for the expression of the Divine to occur. Reuther's words resonate strongly with a sermon I read some years ago given by the previous Archbishop of Canterbury Rowan Williams. At the time I had just taken up a role as a new CEO of an agency working in drug and alcohol rehabilitation and I was talking to a man called John. John told me about his life as a person who had used and misused drugs and alcohol. I was profoundly touched by his story. His story highlighted how easy it seemed in our society to see some people as worthy and others who had 'brought' misfortune on themselves because of their actions, as not worthy. Williams' words resonate with Ruther's injunction that whatever denies, diminishes, or distorts the full humanity of women, and therefore any person, is therefore appraised as not redemptive when he says:

The reverence I owe to every human person is connected with the reverence I owe to God's creative Word, which brings [every human] into being and keeps them in being. I stand before holy ground when I encounter another person – not because they are born with a set of legal rights which they can demand and enforce, but because there is a dimension of their life I shall never fully see; the dimension where they come forth from the purpose of God into the world, with a unique set of capacities and possibilities ... It means that there are no superfluous people, no 'spare' people in the human world. All are needed for the good of all.

These words were transformational for me. Human failure is tragic and terrible because it means that some unique and unrepeatable aspect of God's purpose has not been allowed to flourish. We have no room to allow even one human being to fail. There are none who are not worth fighting for. Whilst one would think that this ought not be a radical view for the Catholic Church, I would suggest that it has become so. This new looking glass that provides a view of the human person has been the core driver for my work, leadership, and advocacy in the social services sector. It is this looking glass that the Plenary Council needs to look through.

Theological reflection and human bodily experience

If the Plenary Council were to be successful, then it would need to hold central the belief that our theological reflection is shaped by our human experience, as people of God and as women. The PC will need to grapple, as we have as women, with how our experience has and continues to be shaped by violence, both within the institutional Church and external to it. The Women in Theology blog writes that as women 'our identities as women have been shaped by violence. *Becoming a woman in our society inevitably entails coming to an acute awareness of bodily vulnerability'.*

If we believe, as I do, that our theological reflections are shaped by our experiences, then as women, and for women, we must speak of these experiences, and name them. We cannot escape nor deny the facts. The truth-telling that is needed in a new Catholic Church must name the facts that face women, facts that are painful to hear, so that we can express our solidarity with those women who are too afraid to speak out (or when they do they feel so alone) who are sitting in our churches silent, too afraid to speak out or who are shamed by religious teaching and practice and clericalism that have blamed women, and used and abused women.

I am mindful that listing the facts is not just an intellectual exercise. It is a sobering deep lament and a sign of solidarity for all women whose bodily experience is not only reflected within our Churches, but also ignored, silenced, and shamefully denied. During the years of the Royal Commission into Institutional Responses to Child Sexual Abuse, I heard only one sermon

...our identities as women have been shaped by violence.

on the topic in my local parish during those years, and even then it was given by a visiting priest. I have heard and read numerous publications on the loudly debated Voluntary Assisted Dying and Abortion issues from our Archdiocese but have heard nothing about violence towards women and their children, one of the biggest social issues of our time. (One woman dies every week in this county at the hand of a current or former partner.) I have heard heated debate over the mandatory reporting of child sexual abuse and the impact on the confessional seal, and yet I have heard nothing addressing the fact that 1 in 5 women in our community have experienced sexual violence since the age of 15. In solidarity with the bodily experience of women let us lament the following:

- On average one woman a week is murdered by her current or former partner.

- First Nations women are 32 times more likely to be hospitalised due to family violence than non-aboriginal women.

- 1 in 4 women have experienced emotional abuse by a current or former partner at some time after the age of 15.

- 1 in 5 women have experienced sexual violence at some time after the age of 15.

- 85% of Australian women have been sexually harassed.

- 92% of women who identify as LGBTQIA+ have experienced sexual harassment in their lifetime.

- 9 out of 10 women with a disability have been sexually harassed.

- 1 in 3 young people presenting alone to homelessness services have experienced domestic violence.
- Domestic and family violence is the leading cause of homelessness for women and children.

> *How can we be so silent about the reality of women's experience in this country, in our Churches?*

No matter how many times I recite this data it still shocks me and runs through my veins like ice. How can we be so silent about the reality of women's experience in this country, in our Churches? Why do our clerics and leaders NOT rail against this in their sermons, in their addresses to the nation?

We often have so many stereotypes of who these women are – pretending they are not like me, not you. But they are. Sharon, a GP from a rural town that was charged with manslaughter of her husband, had survived years of humiliating violence in all its forms at the hand of the man she believed loved her. Kerry – an aboriginal woman, sexually abused as a child and a child victim of family and domestic violence – had cycled in and out of mental health and drug and alcohol services all her life, sleeping rough on the streets and losing her leg due to a circulatory condition brought about by the impact of trauma in her life.

When we as a Church fail to name the lived realities, the experience of women's vulnerability through violence – all forms of violence – then we deny – we silence – the gift that is offered to us in the transformative and relational love that Jesus offers us in his death and resurrection.

Acceptance and embracing of a bodily theology – in particular that of women and the vulnerability of our experience – is one of my hopes for the Plenary Council. I fear that until the Church embraces the bodily revelation of the divine, we will continue to perpetrate and accept the violence that is done to women, and to all those whose bodies do not fit the normative patriarchal paradigm.

My final words of hope for success for the Plenary Council come in the form of a prayer from Janet Morley who reminds us that Christ invites us to intimacy through our bodies, and that the body is to be celebrated when she prays:

O God who took human flesh

That you might be intimate with us

May we so taste and touch you

In our bodily life

That we may discern and celebrate

Your body in the world

Through Jesus Christ Amen

For discussion:

1. Debra comments that 'knowing is always partial, always unfolding and it requires the traveller to be open, to come without judgement'. How should this view apply to the Australian Plenary Council?

2. How can we best 'model the church we want to be, inclusive, diverse, and welcoming'?

3. What is your response to Debra's question: 'How can we be so silent about the reality of women's experience in this country, in our Churches?'

Fear Not!

Good governance and Renewal must arise out of hope not fear; out of humility not arrogance; out of truth not denial.

Robert Fitzgerald AM

Robert Fitzgerald AM was a Royal Commissioner into Institutional Responses to Child Sexual Abuse. Robert has extensive experience in organisational leadership and public and social policy review in the Church and in the government and private sectors. He has been a Commissioner for multiple social policy inquiries in Australia.

Pope John Paul II extolled the faithful: 'Do not be afraid. Do not be satisfied with mediocrity. Put out into the deep and let down your nets for a catch.' It is purported that the Bible contains more than 630 references to 'fear not' or 'be not afraid'. Today, one of the greatest challenges to renewal in our Church is fear. Fear is real, but it is too often exploited by those who seek to resist change and retain the status quo. Whilst it is fear that can paralyse us, it is only hope that can set us free to contemplate the possible in renewing the mission of the gospel and of the Church. Pope Francis calls us to be a people of hope: 'Hope opens new horizons, making us capable of dreaming what is not even imaginable.' Renewal is born out of hope, not fear.

Like so many thousands around Australia, we have collectively entered into the journey of the Fifth Plenary Council of Australia with a genuine hope that a transformed Church can emerge. A new conversation has arisen within the Church and I hope a new dawn for the Church both in this country and beyond will slowly unfold as a consequence.

Reasons for Hope

And there are some sound reasons for hope in Australia. We are a well-educated, considerate, creative and faithful community of Catholics, capable of learning, discerning and renewal. We are proudly egalitarian, seeking fairness and justice in our world and our church. Our clerical, religious and lay leaders are competent and capable of reading 'the signs of the times'. And despite 'nay-sayers' in our church who work tirelessly at undermining reform, we can respond to emerging challenges. Following the Royal Commission into Institutional Responses to Child Sexual Abuse, the Australian Catholic Bishops Conference responded actively to many of its recommendations. In particular, it has strengthened safeguarding and professional standards and importantly commissioned a review of the governance arrangements of the dioceses and parishes.

> *Pope Francis calls us to be a people of hope.*

The resulting report *The Light from the Southern Cross, Promoting Co- Responsible Governance in the Church in Australia* delivered in May 2020 provides great wisdom and guidance in relation to possible reforms within the parish and diocesan contexts. If adopted, the Church would have a sound foundation for the revitalisation of the Church in this nation. Yet, the Church is much more than just dioceses and parishes. It is made up of a myriad of different religious institutions and organisations requiring improved governance. Renewal must be broad and encompassing of the whole of this divine enterprise.

Just as renewal itself arises out of hope so, too, good Church governance must be based in hope not fear. It must be arise out of humility not arrogance. It must be based in truth not denial.

Strengths and Weaknesses today

We do need to acknowledge that evidence, creativity and courage have produced some excellent governance models in parts of Church activity, especially in our works in education, health and social services, for which religious institutes should be justly praised. Whilst there have been these significant advances, there has been little improvement in governance arrangements in dioceses and parishes. Whilst many religious institutes have embraced more accountable, transparent and participatory models of governance, (including the development of ministerial Public Juridic Persons – PJPs) such approaches have not often crossed the aisle into the diocesan and parish structures. Tragically, in some parishes and dioceses we may have even gone backwards.

...poor governance, inadequately formed leadership, inherent conflicts of interest and an unhealthy culture that preferences power, secrecy and the Church's own interests...

Too much of current Church governance is based (intentionally or unintentionally) on a fear of the non-ordained, especially women, a fear of outside influence (even where that is good), and an arrogant assertion of the position of the Church in the world where it maintains the power and privilege of an ordained class. The Church too often dismisses open, transparent, and accountable approaches in favour of secrecy, complexity and legalistic approaches. It embraces systemic gender inequality. It shuns genuine participation. And there are strong forces within the Church that seek not only the status quo but a pre-Vatican II church, preferencing the will and influence of the few, whilst shunning the hopes of the many.

Renewal based on the truth

My personal hopes and aspirations for our church are deeply and profoundly grounded in what I heard, saw and experienced in the recent Royal Commission. It is important to reflect on the truth revealed by those that came forward and the learnings from evidence, research and deep analysis. More importantly, this truth should help inform how we must respond.

As part of the Plenary Council process we have all been called to discernment, yet discernment cannot be authentic if it does not start with a deep understanding of the evidence or truth already revealed. We cannot fear the truth, nor can we ignore it. We must embrace it in order to inform the future.

As the Royal Commission highlighted, poor governance, inadequately formed leadership, inherent conflicts of interest and an unhealthy culture that preferences power, secrecy and the Church's own interests often contributed to the collective failure of the Catholic Church. There was indeed a betrayal of trust, so profound and deep that it called into question the legitimacy and integrity of our church in the eyes of many in our society.

Yet the Church risks further losing the trust and confidence of the people of God and the broader community, unless the

The outcome of good governance is to drive good cultures, support good leadership and build trust in the institution

lessons are learnt, governance is improved and renewal occurs. More specifically the current governance arrangements are increasingly losing legitimacy with the Church's own community of the faithful.

However the Royal Commission is not the reason for change. It only exposed profound weaknesses, that many in church had already raised in recent decades, often to no avail. The calls for renewal were alive well before the Royal Commission and the proposal for the Plenary Council.

As 'The Light from the Southern Cross Report' stated so well:

'The Recommendations in this Report should not be considered just as a response to external circumstances, including the advice of the Royal Commission, but as inherently worthy at this time in the history of the Catholic Church in Australia. They are the right thing to do and the evidence of the submissions to the Fifth Plenary Council for Australia suggest their implementation will be welcomed by the Catholic Community.'

Reform of church governance arrangements, is vital if the Church is to be a relevant, responsive, sacred and transformative body in spreading the Word of God to the faithful and beyond.

The Light from the Southern Cross Report stated, 'The consequences of the governance reform indicated in this report will be a better Church, truer to its mission, more just to all, and embodying the gifts and contribution of all the Peoples of God.'

The outcome of good governance is to drive good cultures, support good leadership and build trust in the institution. It allows the institution's purpose to be fulfilled responsibly, having regard to

Church and societal norms. It allows good practice to be infused with all that is important in our faith-filled mission.

Stewardship models should underpin reforms within the national Church. They should be part of all Church entities including religious institutes and incorporated bodies (including PJPs). Such models can and do give full expression to the mission of the Church in action.

But most importantly they promote integrity, legitimacy, and the just exercise of authority. Too much of current Church governance concentrates on authority, too little on integrity and legitimacy.

Possible practical approaches are emerging as are key principles.

I acknowledge that there are many different ways of articulating principles and governance frameworks. The Light from the Southern Cross Report identifies the key principles, and states them as being collegiality, synodality, subsidiarity, stewardship, dialogue and discernment.

More simply, I propose that good Church governance should be based on five key practical principles which incorporate these themes:

- Legitimacy: the participation of women and men (ordained, religious and lay) in all decision-making processes, giving them voice and responding to those voices. It values relationships of trust, respect and reciprocity, each integral to a synodal model.

- Stewardship: governing for the benefit of God and the faithful, and acting in the best interests of those we serve, as diligent custodians of this divine enterprise.

...intrinsically Catholic in character – mission focussed, values-based, involving the People of God in the shared priesthood that should be the Catholic Church...

- Accountability and transparency: embracing clear lines of responsibility, being accountable for the consequences of decisions, and being open to the church and broader communities in relation to information, data, performance and processes (and their outcomes).

- Performance: developing clearly articulated goals and strategies, using evidence, expertise and appropriate discernment to guide decisions, and openly reviewing and reporting on processes and performance.

- Integrity/faithfulness: acting faithfully, fairly, justly and ethically in all decision making, having regard to church and societal norms and laws. Ensuring a culture and leadership that requires these values to be lived throughout all levels and aspects of the church enterprise, where incentives and values are fully aligned to drive right conduct, behaviours and relationships.

These principles are intrinsically Catholic in character, mission focussed, and values based, involving the People of God in the shared priesthood that should be the Catholic Church.

In practice, what are some real possibilities.

Having regard to those principles following are some preliminary practical approaches that could be considered by the Plenary Council. In many aspects they are

shamefully modest, and far from radical. The Light of the Southern Cross Report made many outstanding recommendations, as have many participating in the Plenary Council processes and the sponsors of this convocation. Nearly all recommendations can be accomplished without any changes to canon law. They can be carried out now. What they do require is the will to do it.

The Plenary Council must not be a process that only leads to lofty rhetoric and broad, vague directions. Practical outcomes, clear timelines, and accountable actions are needed at the end of such a vast process. There are some key practical and achievable proposals to improve governance at all levels that I put forward in this paper.

At national level there is a critical need to enhance participation and stewardship through the following:

- National synods should be held every ten years and diocesan synods every five years involving clerical, religious and lay representation.

- A National Leadership Centre should be established to promote training and formation of all leaders of Church authorities in good governance and stewardship.

- The Church should establish mechanisms, at the national level, to investigate and sanction Church personnel in relation to matters of serious misconduct, removing local conflicts of interest that are inherent in dioceses.

- All ACBC Commissions and Committees should have at least a majority representation by lay persons, with an equal representation of men and women.

- The Church at the national level should develop a standard for public accountability for all levels of the church including the public annual accounting of financial reports, key data and progress updates in relation to strategic plans, commitments arising from synods, pastoral and parish councils, and safeguarding.

At diocesan level there is urgent need for reform. Some reforms are outside the remit of the local church, but the following can be implemented:

- Bishops should be required to act in council, with a small number of ordained, religious and lay (men and women) appointed to a stewardship council, who meet regularly to examine and determine issues of stewardship and the integrity of the diocese. This should sit above all management and other consultative processes and itself be subject to biennial review. Members should not be direct employees of the Bishop.

- All dioceses should have active, ongoing, properly constituted pastoral councils that have fixed terms for individual members, be constituted to survive the change of Bishop, and whilst initially only advisory must be treated as influential. Bishops should be required to respond openly to recommendations and provide reasons if recommendations are not supported.

- Ongoing leadership training and professional development must be put in place for Bishops, members of any stewardship council, and other diocesan decision makers. Ongoing formation should be provided to all pastoral council members and regular reviews of the performance of the council should be undertaken.

- At parish level, the Church is in the process of evolutionary change which must be underpinned by improved governance and lay participation.

- New models of parish governance and management should be developed to allow for team-based ministries with parish leadership by lay, religious or ordained based on suitability, skills and experience – not status.

- Parishes should be required to establish purposeful, properly constituted parish councils with appropriate representation of the parish community, fixed terms for individuals, and clearly articulated delegated responsibilities. Whilst priests should continue to have overall responsibilities for the spiritual and sacramental direction and wellbeing of the parish they should willingly and actively delegate ministerial responsibilities to appropriately trained and formed persons.

- All priests and members of parish councils should be required to undertake ongoing stewardship training and formation, and the performance of the parish council and governance of the parish should be regularly monitored and transparently undertaken.

Within religious institutes and other entities the journey to good governance continues.

- Religious orders and congregations should ensure their leadership teams undergo appropriate stewardship training and that reviews of their governance arrangements, good stewardship and performance generally should be undertaken every few years. External personnel should be engaged to conduct such reviews.

- All boards and advisory bodies of Church entities – including school councils – should be representative of men and women, have fixed terms for members and all members should be required to undertake ongoing stewardship training and formation.

- All boards and advisory councils of Church entities should undertake a biennial review focussing on their commitment to good governance

- Where a Church entity has a board, without an active membership to which it is accountable, serious consideration should be given to establishing a small stewardship board to oversight issues of integrity and stewardship.

More than governance

Of course governance improvements sit within a broader set of issues confronting the Church. To name a few that are needed: an ongoing improvement of safeguarding policies and processes; reducing unhealthy clericalism, especially in seminaries; reviewing the selection, formation, training and ongoing supervision of ordained and religious; removing mandatory celibacy requirements within the diocesan priesthood; increasing the role and voice of women and removing systemic gender inequality; greater consultation in relation to the appointment of Bishops and parish priests and, where necessary, changes to canon law.

The emerging agenda of the Plenary Council provides a broad, rich, and diverse suite of issues which will challenge, confront, encourage and give hope, provided the process is authentic in giving voice to the People of God.

Towards a revitalised future.

The words of the authors of The Light from the Southern Cross should be heeded.

'This Report then is intended as encouragement to those who exercise power and authority in the Catholic community to see the structures and law in a way that enhances and supports rather than inhibits, the mission and life of that community. The Report seeks to support the prophetic nature of the missionary church by examining and suggesting changes in governance and management that build on its structures in a positive way.'

'The object of this Review is to encourage church leaders to locate their canonical authority within the framework of co-responsibility with the whole community of the baptised. Such collaboration will benefit all of God's people and will contribute positively to the good of the society in which the Gospel message is to be proclaimed.'

We have the capacity to reshape our institutions and the Church at large:

- To create a church that is genuinely safe for children and vulnerable adults and which acts in their best interests, listens deeply to them and provides healing and hope.

- To create a church whose governance and leadership is participatory, competent, engaged and open to evidence, learning and improvement, inspired and infused by the Holy Spirit.

- To create an ongoing conversation with the people of God and to genuinely invite them into the governance of the Church, where reciprocity and mutual respect underpin right relations.

- To create a church more truthful, transparent and accountable to the faithful and the community at large in which trust can be restored.

- To create a church authentically based on the Gospel and the revelations of Jesus Christ – one that seeks to heal not to hurt, to include not to exclude, to nurture not control.

The Plenary Council process has opened up the Church community to a new way of conversation and discernment that highlights but transcends division. Today, in this nation, there is a compelling need for genuine reciprocity across the Church community, based on mutual respect and the valuing of diverse beliefs, in a spirit that seeks acceptance not division. A future in which there can be a celebration of diversity of skills, talents, views and practices, with a common, unshakeable belief in God and his mission and within a universal church infused by the gifts of the Holy Spirit. We can do it!

For discussion:

1. Robert observes: 'A new conversation has arisen within the Church and I hope a new dawn for the Church both in this country and beyond will slowly unfold as a consequence.' What are your hopes for the Plenary Council in considering the failings in the Church's governance?

2. '(The Church) too often dismisses open, transparent and accountable approaches in favour of secrecy, complexity and legalistic approaches.' How should the Plenary Council address this?

3. How can lay Catholics have a role in 'reshap(ing) our institutions and the Church at large'?

Governance improvements sit within a broader set of issues confronting the Church...

Towards and Beyond the Council

John Warhurst

John Warhurst AO is an Emeritus Professor of the Australian National University, Chair of Concerned Catholics Canberra Goulburn and a Plenary Council member. John writes regularly for Eureka Street and the Canberra Times. He was a member of the writing team for The Light from the Southern Cross, the report on Church governance commissioned by the Australian bishops.

The Plenary Council: Knowns and Unknowns

When the second Convocation of Catholics was held on August 26, 2021 the Plenary Council was only weeks away. There was still much to learn about how it would operate in practice but the broad outline was known.

The history of the Plenary Council should not be forgotten, nor should we forget the largely unsuccessful efforts by reformers to make it more inclusive. This history is a testament to the energy for reform demonstrated by those Catholics who have engaged with the process, but that process has been firmly top-down and exclusive rather than inclusive. The energy for reform shown in the 17,500 submissions made in the early stages of the process is largely absent from the final Plenary Council document, the PC Agenda Questions.

The history frames the approach of reformers to the Plenary Council. Since the early days of the process we have walked a fine line between being rightly critical of its limitations and engaging with it positively in every way that we can. We have never seen it as the only, or even the main, opportunity to reform our church, but we have made the judgement that it is an opportunity too good to overlook. We now know the fruits of our efforts and can deal with the situation which presents itself warts and all.

The shape of the Plenary Council to which our efforts today have been directed has five elements.

First, it will operate under Vatican rules. That is, the official Statutes and Regulatory Norms define its operations. They... have been published and have been explained to the PC members by Fr Stephen Hackett, General Secretary of the Australian Catholic Bishops Conference.

An opportunity too good to overlook.

The main relevant aspects of these rules include the general composition and voting rules of the assembly as well as its legislative powers. The composition was amended by negotiation between Australia and the Vatican to include more lay members, but the representation of the laity is still insufficient. There are two types of votes: deliberative votes held by bishops and consultative votes held by non-episcopal members. Legislation, once carried by a majority of the deliberative votes, applies, like Canon Law, to the life of the church in Australia.

Secondly, the final composition is 282 members, including 47 bishops and 235 non-episcopal members. The general composition, heavily weighted towards male bishops and clerics, severely under-represents women and lay men, but the overall composition is still diverse.

The leadership, the President Archbishop Tim Costelloe and the Vice-President, Bishop Shane

The general composition, heavily weighted towards male bishops and clerics, severely under-represents women and lay men

MacKinlay, is male, as is the Bishops' Commission for the Plenary Council. The PC Executive Committee, the PC Facilitation Team including the team leader, Ms Lana Turvey-Collins, and the facilitators are gender balanced.

Thirdly, the guiding methodology is that of Spiritual Conversations, sometimes known as Deep Listening or Ignatian Spirituality. This method is structured, and the contribution of each participant is not just encouraged but demanded.

Fourthly, rather than gathering in the one physical location, the PC members will be home-based or in small local groups from which they will work virtually with others across the country. Once a day there will be a two-hour online plenary session involving all members.

> *...the PC business meetings will be conducted over just six days...*

Finally, the PC business meetings will be conducted over just six days so the agenda will be crowded. There is a three-hour time difference, because of daylight saving, between the east and west coasts, which creates a further pressure on time.

Within this general format there are several unknowns.

The first relates to the dynamics of the assembly. We await further information than is contained in the Statutes and Regulatory Norms about the 'standing orders' covering detailed agenda items, speaking from the floor, moving and seconding motions and bringing motions to a vote.

The second relates to the question of how the Assembly members relate to the wider Catholic community. This includes practical matters such as the distribution to members of suggestions from the community.

Members were told, during one of the Formation sessions, that the Assembly would be a community but not a bubble. Those helpful images are of great importance in assessing how the community can best support Assembly members and how members can best listen to the community.

Convocation 2 Speakers

The purpose of the second convocation was to address hopes and aspirations for the Plenary Council, including some of the key PC questions. In this convocation we heard the wisdom of five speakers.

Dr Miriam Rose Ungunmerr Baumann offered a powerful perspective on the changes in the church which are necessary for a First Nations leader. Her insights into First Nations' spirituality taught us about 'Dadirri' – inner deep listening and quiet, and still awareness. Listening to Indigenous spirituality should not merely be an outcome of the Plenary Council but it should inform the Council's approach to discernment of the Holy Spirit and spiritual conversation.

Dr Ungunmerr Baumann offered several concrete proposals, which might open up for PC members the PC Agenda Question 3: 'How might the Church in Australia open in new ways to Indigenous ways of being Christian in spirituality, theology, liturgy and missionary discipleship? How might we learn from the First Nations peoples?'

This question should be a leading priority of the PC. Answering it will require deeply listening to Indigenous members of the council and other Indigenous Catholic leaders and communities, while being conscious of the voice of established Indigenous Catholic agencies at various levels of the church, including the

National Aboriginal and Torres Strait Islander Catholic Council (NATSICC).

The very presence of Robert Fitzgerald AM emphasised the importance of the PC recognising the role of the Royal Commission into Institutional Responses to Child Sexual Abuse in unveiling the crisis in the church. As a former commissioner, Fitzgerald's view of the continuing lessons of the Royal Commission for the future of the church in Australia is crucial. The Light from the Southern Cross, the official Church report on governance, owed its genesis to the recommendations of the Royal Commission about the cultural and governance failures of the Church which contributed both to the crimes of child sexual abuse and to its criminal concealment by church leaders.

In considering the PC Agenda questions, including Qusetion 14, 'How might we recast governance at every level of the Church in Australia in a more missionary key?' Fitzgerald offered us general wisdom informed by his admiration for The Light from the Southern Cross report, and hope and confidence that the Catholic community, well-educated, considerate, creative and faithful, possessed the capacity for successful reform of the Church.

He offered concrete proposals to the national level and to dioceses, parishes and religious institutes. They were based on five key practical principles: legitimacy, stewardship, accountability and transparency, performance and integrity and faithfulness. At the national level the proposals included national synods every ten years, while at the diocesan level they included synods every five years and active, ongoing and properly constituted pastoral councils. Also, parishes should include team-based ministries and pastoral councils.

One of the most powerful driving forces behind Church reform is the desire for equality for women in the decision-making of the church. Debra Zanella, drawing on the contributions of Sister Joan Chittister, documented discrimination against women within the Church. Her wide range of experience in modern society working with those at the margins of society informed her remarks. She spoke to the experience of women, LGBTQI people and Aboriginal people.

Zanella sought a church which is inclusive, diverse and welcoming; one that is not based on a patriarchal normative experience and one which embraces a New Theology. Her new Catholic Church, quoting John Carroll, would embrace 'full democratic reform' with no equivocation or half-measures. This new church must recognise the violence against women and its leaders must be willing to speak up about it in sermons and addresses to the nation.

Truth-telling in the new church must face and name the painful facts that confront women, one in five of whom have experienced sexual violence after the age of 15. These women are sitting in our church pews silently and must be given a voice by the church.

Many of the matters being discussed at the Plenary Council have a universal context. Pope Francis has led the way towards a synodal church operating with co-responsibility between its clerical and lay members. He has encouraged the voice of the laity and his approach to synods of bishops has encouraged developments around the world, including the Plenary Council in Australia.

Inspired by Pope Francis, synods and assemblies are underway or being considered in many countries and regions of the world, including the Amazon, Germany, Ireland and the United Kingdom. Reformers in the Church in Australia value international connections and learn from the wider perspectives that such observers can bring.

An Agenda for Reform: ACCCR Response to the PC Agenda Questions

The speakers at Convocation 2 offered their own perspectives which related to the PC Agenda Questions. Together they made a powerful contribution, echoing the aspirations of many reforming Catholics.

Concurrently the Australasian Catholic Coalition for Church Reform (ACCCR), the sponsor of the Convocations, composed its own comprehensive response to the invitation to the Catholic community to offer concrete proposals for consideration by the Plenary Council. This response is included in this booklet, which will be distributed to all PC members.

This PC call for concrete proposals suffered from several distinct limitations, which complicated the task before the ACCCR.

First, in the words of the ACCCR, the PC agenda 'offers limited scope for necessary and wide-ranging reform and renewal', in part because it 'suggests an unrealistic picture of our Church with little recognition of its current perilous state'.

Secondly, it neglects the thousands of concrete proposals already submitted by the People of God within the 17,500 submissions and in some cases within the reports of the PCs own six Writing and Discernment groups. Much of great benefit has been forgotten and lost in distillation and generalisation.

Thirdly, the call lacks any guidance as to what general form a concrete proposal should take. The guidance might have offered advice on what level of detail would be appropriate, in other words what level of concreteness, whether general proposals or specific programs of actions.

Bearing that in mind, the response offered by the ACCCR comprises different types of proposal from the absolutely specific to the more general. The following proposals are some examples:

Absolutely Specific:

- Endorse the Uluru Statement from the Heart.
- Require Inclusive Language to be used in all church liturgies.
- Pursue with the Holy See the ordination to the priesthood of women and married men.
- Adopt *Laudato Si'* as a blueprint for leadership and action.
- Legislate for the establishment of Diocesan Pastoral Councils in each diocese and Parish Pastoral Councils in each parish.

More General:

- Resolve the Australian bishops fund social housing initiatives.
- Require each diocese and parish to adopt and make publicly available a plan for practical engagement with other Christian churches and communities of other faiths.

Quite General:

- Promote liturgical diversity.
- Affirm the role of personal conscience.
- Adopt, as a core principle, engagement in social action on behalf of marginalised and vulnerable people as an authentic expression of faith on a par with regular Mass attendance.

Conclusion

The Plenary Council is entering a period of intense activity that will discern the future of the Church in Australia. The Catholic community has invested great hopes in the outcomes and will hold its leaders to account if our hopes are disappointed.

The reform movement has offered both the Convocations of Catholics series and detailed responses to the PC Agenda Questions. Big picture ideas and concrete proposals sit side by side and reinforce one another.

We should see these Convocation contributions and the observations and proposals from the ACCCR as yet another iteration and not, by any means, the final one. Our critique of the PC First Assembly will generate more responses. We should be prepared to offer several more sets of suggestions from immediately after the First PC Assembly until the Second Assembly in July 2022 and beyond. Even that will not be enough. We will need to follow ongoing discussion and implementation closely for years to come.

For discussion:

1. John observes: 'The Plenary Council is entering a period of intense activity, discerning the future of the Church in Australia.' What do you see as the major challenges facing the members of the Plenary Council: bishops, clerics, religious and lay people – women and men?

2. The Australasian Catholic Coalition for Church Reform considers that the Plenary Council agenda 'offers limited scope for necessary and wide-ranging reform and renewal', in part because it 'suggests an unrealistic picture of our Church with little recognition of its current perilous state'. Do you regard the Agenda questions as 'fit for purpose'? (The Agenda questions are included in the next chapter)

The Plenary Council

A Response to the Plenary Council Agenda 3-10 October 2021 with Concrete Proposals

Australasian Catholic Coalition for Church Reform

Executive Summary

Our Church is at a crisis point, no longer adequately inspiring our people. We Catholics desire a 'grown-up' Church and recognise that the necessary reform requires major cultural change. All of us have a right and a responsibility to be engaged in this renewal. Relevant, constructive, and concrete proposals and actions are needed now more than ever to shape our Church for the task of proclaiming the vision and mission of Jesus in the 21st century.

We are concerned that the Agenda questions for the Plenary Council do not encourage serious examination of the deep-seated issues underlying the numerous challenges facing thinking Catholics. We do not endorse the Agenda as it is and request that it be replaced. We urge those Members of the Plenary Council who have a similar view on the inadequacy of the current PC Agenda, to express that view prior to, or at the outset of the first session, and in the strongest possible terms.

However, with a desire to work synodally, we offer our observations and proposals on the Agenda without being constrained by its restricted perspective. Key themes in our response include:

- Inclusion, the elimination of all forms of discrimination in our Church in relation to sharing Eucharist, providing pastoral care, or sacramental ministry, and particularly of women, LGBTIQA+ people;

- Implementation of the recommendations of The Light from the Southern Cross report, particularly sections on:

  – Identification of the Principles and Culture of Good Governance, and

  – Good Governance Practices and Culture using auditable timelines;

- The concerns and spiritual perceptions of First Nations people;

- Sensitive and just support for the survivors of sexual abuse, refugees and asylum seekers, and marginalised people, and advocating for fundamental change in public policies that cause or enable vulnerability and disadvantage;

- The eradication of clericalism in all its forms, while working towards new pathways to ministry for all, including women and married men;

- Implementation of Diocesan Pastoral Councils and Parish Pastoral Councils in every Australian diocese and parish;

- The need for a major paradigm shift involving deep change, new modes of leadership both clerical and lay, and structures which ensure accountability, transparency and inclusion, especially of women in all leadership and decision-making;

- Examination of the traditional concept of 'parish' to consider smaller, more intimate groups of Catholics as the basic structure of the local Church;

- Synodality, recognising that all Catholics have gifts, talents and expertise for leadership; together we form a priestly people, requiring quality formation opportunities;

- The adoption of Pope Francis' encyclical Laudato Si' and the principles of integral ecology as blueprints for Church action, leadership and advocacy in caring for our environment;

- The imperative that those matters that are beyond the competence of Australian bishops be referred to the Holy See.

The Plenary Council has the potential to be a catalyst, a fulcrum on which an emerging Church can pivot towards the future. It could be a significant step towards a recovered vision of God's revelation in Jesus and the Spirit within faith communities and in transforming our world and creation.

We call on Plenary Council members to respond to Pope Francis' hopes for a new era of synodality and accountability where we all walk humbly together. It will require uncommon courage and a commitment to changes in how we do and are church. For this to happen, we must be open to radical conversion, reform, and renewal. Let us journey in the Spirit!

Introduction

Our Church is at a crisis point, no longer adequately inspiring our people. In an interview with the BBC, Archbishop Coleridge, President of the Australian Catholic Bishops Conference, admitted, 'the credibility of the church is shot to pieces'. Asked to explain this comment, he said, 'It's true but up to a point because our agencies retain great credibility but it is the bishops overwhelmingly who have lost credibility.' The Archbishop of Melbourne, with the largest Catholic population in Australia, recently stated that his diocese is on a 'threshold' and either we do something or 'sink into the sunset'.

The institutional Church has alienated many people who for years lived a sacramental life, including many who attended Catholic schools. It has now become irrelevant to the lives of too many of our people.

After almost 60 years, our Church is not yet a Vatican II institution, a truly collegial Church in which decisions respect local cultures, communities and circumstances. Rather, its activities are often based on legalism and control, with inadequate listening and dialogue, and often over-focused on its institutional image.

The Royal Commission into Institutional Responses to Child Sexual Abuse has not only condemned the horror of child sexual abuse by clerics but has censured bishops for covering up that abuse

The Royal Commission into Institutional Responses to Child Sexual Abuse has not only condemned the horror of child sexual abuse by clerics but has censured bishops for covering up that abuse and exposing

children to harm. This response is a demonstration of the autocratic and unaccountable clericalist decision-making that pervades our Church's leadership. In a *Letter to all Catholics*, Pope Francis wrote,

> To say 'no' to abuse is to say an emphatic 'no' to all forms of clericalism. Clericalism, involves trying to replace or silence or ignore or reduce the people of God to small elites. (August 20, 2018).

The Plenary Council must respond to Pope Francis' hopes for a new era of synodality, and create a Church that listens to a range of voices. This church must be a model of the church that Jesus expects from us in this millennium, and one that will require changes on how we do and are church. This requires radical conversion, reform and renewal.

The Introduction to the Plenary Council Agenda sets out the task for the Plenary Council members: 'to develop concrete proposals to create a more missionary, Christ-centred Church in Australia at this time.' It goes on to spell out the 'missionary option', quoting Pope Francis in stating it should be: 'a missionary impulse capable of transforming everything ... for the evangelisation of today's world rather than for her self-preservation. (*Evangelii Gaudium* n.2)

This is not a time to be faint-hearted about the task ahead. Deep discernment is needed by all the members of the Plenary Council. The process and deliberations of the Plenary Council must focus on Jesus' vision and mission, our inspiration, and positive outcomes for the people of God. A major paradigm shift is required as we aspire to being a holy people rather than just a church-going people.

Since the outcomes of the Plenary Council will affect all of us who care about our Church, every Catholic also needs to be attentive

to the voice of the Spirit in our reflections and deliberations on this important task. It is for us to understand and apply the vision and message of Jesus to the here and now. Our decisions are to be assessed against the criterion of bringing the good news of Jesus to our own lives, our communities and society; the news that is most clearly exemplified in Jesus' own life. The responsible course of action then is to make our views known to Plenary Council members.

However, it is extremely disappointing that the *Agenda* which the bishops have decided upon does not show that it has arisen from the discernment process that they established. It appears to ignore the priorities that thousands of Catholics distilled from their many deliberations and expressed so clearly in their submissions. It does not even reflect the narrow prospects for change implied in the *Instrumentum Laboris* that we were told would shape the Agenda, and it offers limited scope for necessary and wide-ranging reform and renewal. This agenda seems designed towards moderating existing policies and structures at best, and in ways that provide for an appearance of renewal rather than substantial reform.

The Agenda as presented suggests an unrealistic picture of our Church with little recognition of its current perilous state. The agenda items and questions do not encourage consideration of the real issues. Further, it seems to try to discourage consideration of matters outside the narrow legislative competence of Australian bishops. We do not endorse the *Agenda* as it is and request that it be replaced. We urge those Members of the Plenary Council who have a similar view on the inadequacy of the current PC Agenda to express that view prior to, or at the outset of the first session, in the strongest possible terms.

However, with a desire to make the Plenary Council as productive an exercise in synodality as is possible, we have not been constrained by its restricted perspective, as expressed in our observations. As the Introduction to the *Agenda* states, the task for the Plenary Council members is *'to develop concrete proposals to create a more missionary, Christ-centred Church in Australia at this time.'* The members also must not be constrained in this task by accepting the limitations of these narrow *Agenda Questions*.

We, the members of the nineteen Catholic organisations which make up the Australasian Catholic Coalition for Church Reform (ACCCR), reach out to the members of the Plenary Council, recognising their most important role in ensuring the Council's success and building the Australian Church of the future. We have carefully considered the questions that make up the Plenary Council Agenda and we share our thoughts on some critical aspects. (We have numbered the sixteen Agenda Questions within the six themes as Agenda Questions 1-16 for ease of reference.)

In responding to each question as presented, we first provide observations on the experience of Catholics and the Church community that we seek to be and to personify in our living, noting the extended context within which the issues arise. A community's missionary impulse is *'the fruit of its own experience'* (EG n.24).

Relevant, constructive, concrete proposals are identified in seeking to renew our Church as Christ-centred and missionary. These insights and concerns represent the sense of faith of the Australian faithful and a desire for a 'grown-up' Church. Real reform is going to involve major cultural change. We seek to be part of the movement that leads to and through this change.

Inclusion, equality of women and men, clericalism and the opening of all ministries, including ordination for women and married men are major concerns for everyone we have consulted in preparing this response. These were also dominant themes in the submissions to the Plenary Council.

Some proposals apply to more than one agenda item and are repeated as appropriate. In particular, the recommendations of The Light from the Southern Cross report, commissioned by the Australian Catholic Bishops Conference in response to the Royal Commission's criticism of the Church's governance, are applicable to all questions. Renewal of our Church cannot be achieved without reforming the Church's leadership methods, governance, and culture, all addressed with considerable wisdom in The Light from the Southern Cross. *Getting Back on Mission: Reforming Our Church Together* by Catholics for Renewal is also valuable in this regard.

The people of the Church and indeed the Pope, in his commitment to synodality, expect that the concerns of Australian Catholics should be identified and made known to the competent authorities, especially in matters beyond the jurisdiction of local bishops. The Plenary Council should advise the Holy See of those issues of the Australian Church that are beyond the competence of the Australian bishops.

These observations and proposals are presented to the members of the Plenary Council as an expression of hope and trust arising from the experience of Australian Catholics. Let the voices of the people be heard!

The Plenary Council should advise the Holy See of those issues of the Australian Church that are beyond the competence of the Australian bishops.

Plenary Council Agenda Questions

Conversion

AGENDA QUESTION 1:

How might we better accompany one another on the journey of personal and communal conversion which mission in Australia requires?

Our Observations

Conversion is foundational. Integrity, authenticity, a good conscience, and love for all people and God's creation are the hallmarks of true Christian conversion. Maturity means internalising and taking responsibility for one's own development, values and actions, not just following the beckoning of 'authorities'. This is a sure and firm basis for reaching out to others.

All Catholics share in the full membership of the Church. Ordination to any particular ministry does not make a person more Christian or more Catholic and does not take away from or diminish the freedom of others to act according to their consciences, to express their personal beliefs and to live as they discern best for themselves. It is not for another to judge whether or not individuals should receive communion, how they settle their living arrangements or how frequently they attend Mass.

Many Catholics are now very well educated, well read, people of the world with experience of diverse peoples and cultures. They are leaders in health, education, the law, politics, the sciences, among many other fields. They think critically and are prepared to question and discuss a broad range of topics including issues of faith. Many are better educated than the ordained. In short, they have a broad and deep life experience which sits at the core of understanding and they are living the words

and example of Jesus. Many of us have the Catholic education system to thank for this. As the majority of Catholics now assert, life is primarily about caring for your family and getting your life organised. It is about appreciating the wonders of the natural and human world. It is about creativity in art and culture, caring relationships, doing well in your occupation, trade or profession and fostering critical enquiry and personal integrity.

Christian communities ought to be characterised by a welcoming supportive attitude, personal relationships, care and concern for one another, and inclusive of all the people of God, i.e., all people, without discrimination – according to lifestyle, gender, sexual orientation, etc. Discrimination against women, LGBTIQA+ people, and re-partnered people are the most blatant examples of discrimination in our Church, but not the only ones. Pope Francis says in Let Us Dream that our main task is not to disengage from differences, but to engage in conflict and disagreement in ways that prevent us from descending into polarisation.

Civil society has already held our Church to account over the clerical sexual abuse of children and its cover-up. Still, there is inadequate attention to the voices of victims and survivors. And the Church has failed to address the dysfunctional governance and culture that facilitated the cover-up by Church leaders. The perceived gap between many of the positions and practices of the Church and the gospel of Jesus is a scandal to many, presenting the Church as hypocritical and a negative force in society. We cannot persist in believing so many are wrong in following their consciences and best instincts in this. Reform is required to ensure a truly Christian Church in all its leadership, teachings and practices.

Joseph Ratzinger, later Pope Benedict XVI, wrote in 1968:

Over the Pope as the expression of the binding claim of ecclesiastical authority there still stands one's own conscience, which must be obeyed before all else, if necessary, even against the requirement of ecclesiastical authority. Conscience confronts [the individual] with a supreme and ultimate tribunal, and one which in the last resort is beyond the claim of external social groups, even of the official church.

Pope Francis stated in *Amoris Laetitia* that the Church is 'called to form consciences, not replace them'. Now is the time for the hierarchy to listen to the judgement of the people, to the sense of faith of the faithful. As a Church all of us, not just our leaders, should model the values we teach and recognise the work of the Spirit in every person.

Proposals

That the Plenary Council:

1. Affirm the critical role of personal conscience as the basis and authentication for an inner voice and authority in relation to conversion and how we conduct our living, how we grow and shape a responsible self and the relationships in which we engage;

2. Recognise the work of the Spirit in all of God's people;

3. Acknowledge the full dignity of women and LGBTIQA+ peoples;

4. Recognise and seek to understand the position of the vast majority of Catholics on matters such as family planning and contraception, relationship breakdown and cohabiting,

sexual ethics, justice for sexual and gender diverse people and all LGBTIQA+ people in reviewing Catholic teaching;

5. Commit to the elimination of all forms of discrimination and exclusion from our Church, whether in relation to sharing Eucharist, providing pastoral care, or sacramental ministry;

6. Promote and establish the core elements of Christianity – love and care as the way to a worthwhile life and a better world, and life as larger than biological death – as the criteria for all Church activities;

7. Ensure that personal and community formation opportunities are available and accessible in every diocese and parish;

8. Establish guidelines and inform clergy on how they should advise those who, in good conscience, need to use contraception in their family planning, need to be in relationships after marriage breakdown, or are in stable same-sex relationships;

9. Promote small groups (basic communities) as essential key places of mutual support, learning and evangelisation.

AGENDA QUESTION 2:

How might we heal the wounds of abuse through coming to see through the eyes of those who have been abused?

Our Observations

Conversion of love for the person abused, hurt and damaged comes before and underpins the motivation for action. With the eyes and insights of love, the interests of the victims are paramount. The calling of the Plenary Council was in large part a response to the Royal Commission into Institutional Response to Child Sexual Abuse. This reality needs to be recognised.

Complaints abound about the slow rate of response to victims. We will know that we are doing something right when we hear them telling us so publicly.

And let us never forget all those other Catholics who have suffered other forms of abuse by clergy and hierarchy when no respect was shown to them and they were denied the dignity of God's people.

We note that women suffer continuous abuse in our Church, including through exclusion from positions of responsibility and influence by their God-given gender.

Proposals

That the Plenary Council:

1. Invite victims and survivors to have a voice at the Plenary Council;

2. Promote development of liturgical expressions of lament;

3. Ensure speedy, effective and transparent compliance with the National Redress Scheme;

4. Ensure the independence of any future complaints handling scheme by entrusting all its juridical functions — investigative, adjudicative, and redress — to institutions which are structurally separate from, but funded by, the Church.

5. Commit to accountability, transparency and inclusion in relation to all claims of abuse;

6. Adopt the relevant recommendations of the Royal Commission;

7. Develop ministries to work with abused people to help them overcome their deep sense of spiritual harm;

8. Initiate a direct conversation between the bishops, Catholic social service agencies and support and advocacy organisations to develop and implement a quality healing strategy and undertake the construction of Gardens of Healing;

9. Propose the appointment of two full-time chaplains, one female and one male, for sexual abuse survivors within the chaplaincy and caring framework of Catholic social services in each diocese;

10. Develop a structured network of support groups and an individualised befriending support program for sexual abuse survivors.

AGENDA QUESTION 3:

How might the Church in Australia open in new ways to Indigenous ways of being Christian in spirituality, theology, liturgy, and missionary discipleship? How might we learn from the First Nations peoples?

Our Observations

Aboriginal spirituality and Dreaming have much to offer in their parallels with Catholic traditions and our scriptural inheritance. This spiritual culture grounded in and emerging from the experience of 60,000 years, is an authentic communication of God from which the Church has much to learn.

The initiative of Bishop Samuel Ruiz of Chiapas, Mexico, in ordaining hundreds of indigenous permanent deacons and undertaking other related initiatives in Latin America provides valuable lessons on what is possible and what is successful.

Proposals

That the Plenary Council:

1. Listen to the concerns and spiritual understandings of Australian First Nations peoples;

2. Propose that First Nations peoples' artefacts and acknowledgement plaques be displayed in churches, schools and other relevant buildings and where appropriate, incorporate ATSI designs into vestments and church furnishings;

3. Encourage First Nations peoples to create liturgies, including Eucharistic celebrations, that incorporate or reflect elements of Indigenous spirituality and heritage, and seek their participation in parish education programs and decision-making;

4. Develop an Australian Rite which expresses our unique circumstances, our heritage of First Nations peoples' spirituality, acknowledges our history of dispossession and take-over and continuing racism and envisions a future of respect for everyone;

5. Endorse the 'Statement From The Heart' and have it in prominent public display in churches and school buildings;

6. Incorporate First Nations location names into all parishes, schools and relevant Church locations;

7. Teach local First Nations peoples' history and belief as part of all formation courses;

8. Promote and properly fund the creation of a Centre for Aboriginal Theology and Spirituality;

9. Encourage the ordination of First Nations people.

AGENDA QUESTION 4A:

How might the Church in Australia meet the needs of the most vulnerable, go to the peripheries, and be missionary in places that may be overlooked or left behind in contemporary Australia?

Our Observations

Social services are at the heart of what it is to be Christian. Catholics are to be found in all places on the edge, much of their Christian service done informally. Catholic agencies, for the most part, have a positive profile in this area, as do chaplains and members of Religious Congregations of both men and women. However, Church leadership is still often perceived as self-serving and exclusivist rather than committed to the well-being of those on the peripheries.

To complement the hands-on work and provide for long-term, permanent solutions to the needs of the most vulnerable, our political system must promote policies and programs such as a just economy, a liveable level of social security, citizenship for asylum seekers and realistic action on climate change. Otherwise agencies are engaged in repetitive bandaid struggles. The poor are always there waiting as the mirrors of our own brokenness and the face of a deeply involved and compassionate God. The Church must not only tend to the vulnerable but seek fundamental changes to those aspects of our society that cause vulnerability and disadvantage.

The institutional Church needs to be aware that it sometimes impedes the work of God's people in these endeavours because of avoidable negative perceptions and intolerant attitudes.

Proposals

That the Plenary Council:

1. Adopt, as a core principle, engagement in social action on and with marginalised and vulnerable people as an authentic expression of faith complementary to Mass attendance;

2. Resolve that bishops, clergy and laity reject authority and status and walk humbly with one another to serve needs with our leaders seen to be engaged with those on the edge, avoiding token or liturgical gestures. All leaders should have regular (not short and token) work as frontline service providers under the direction and leadership of appropriately skilled professionals;

3. Resolve that the Church, particularly those in leadership positions, strive to model the best of Christian behaviour in seeking to influence the society we live in, including in the principles of human dignity, common good, subsidiarity and solidarity and the promotion in practice of equality, inclusion and accountability;

4. Recognise and emphasise that lay Catholics have the same gifts, talents and expertise for leadership in the Church as the ordained; all sharing responsibility for promoting and acting for the good of all God's people.

5. Resolve that the Church at all levels work for political change in relation to public policies and programs that are both timely and effective, including the social justice principles set forth in 3 above that affect the poor and marginalised, and, as often as possible in collaboration with broader community networks including all faith communities;

6. Resolve that the bishops fund social housing initiatives, especially in indigenous areas requiring bishops to use Church resources, such as surplus land, towards actualising recommendations of Social Justice Statements.

AGENDA QUESTION 4B:

How might we partner with others (Christians, people of other faiths, neighbourhood community groups, government) to do this?

Our Observations

Christianity demands collaboration of its various communities and traditions in the promotion of the way of Jesus. Christians also have much in common with other religions in relation to perspectives, values and forms of action. There is already a significant level of cooperation in many areas, such as social justice, environmental and climate change issues, education and religious celebrations. This is a foundation to be built upon and developed for the more explicit promotion of the way of love, mutual care and a better world.

As Australia becomes more secular and more multi-faith with growing numbers of migrants bringing their own traditions, the experience of Catholics in countries where Christianity is a minority religion, particularly in Asia, could provide significant learning opportunities for our Church

Proposals

That the Plenary Council:

1. Stipulate that every diocese and parish adopt and make publicly available a plan for practical engagement and cooperation with other Christian churches and communities of other faiths;

2. Stress that our leaders be seen beyond token or liturgical gestures to respect and be engaged with other Christian churches and people of other faiths, beyond token or liturgical gestures;

3. Stress that the Eucharist is 'food for the journey' for all;

4. Resolve that dioceses and parishes create partnerships and groups to actively pursue ecumenism and mutual respect amongst all religions as we seek to do the will of God;

5. Require all prayer forms and liturgies to explicitly recognise the truth and value in other Christian churches and other faiths.

6. Encourage Australian bishops to liaise with their Asian counterparts, e.g. the ACBC with the Federation of Asian Bishops' Conferences (FABC).

AGENDA QUESTION 5:

How might the Church in Australia respond to the call to 'ecological conversion'? How can we express and promote a commitment to an 'integral ecology of life' in all its dimensions, with particular attention to the more vulnerable people and environments in our country and region?

Our Observations

Climate is truly one of the major moral issues of our times and has to be addressed at personal, community, national and global levels.

Many individuals, family groups and school communities already participate in Laudato Si' events and other initiatives addressing climate change. But there is no universal response to all that Pope Francis proposes in his encyclical.

Integral ecology affirms the interrelationship of all aspects of life and existence. Liturgies, especially Eucharistic liturgies, could be developed to reflect this. Likewise, promoting ecological sustainability is a central Christian responsibility.

Proposals

That the Plenary Council:

1. Adopt Pope Francis' encyclical *Laudato Si'* as a blueprint for Church leadership, advocacy and behaviour in caring for our environment, and give it priority and facilitate it by resourcing activists and advocates;

2. Stipulate that every diocese and parish develop and publish a strategy for taking practical, auditable steps to reduce their carbon footprint, e.g. solar panels on all Church buildings, schools, and other facilities;

3. Stipulate that every diocese and parish develop relevant education programs, liturgies, homilies and parish mission statements;

4. Endorse advocacy and lobbying in the public square for renewable energy as we move away from reliance on carbon and polluting fuels.

Prayer

AGENDA QUESTION 6:

How might we become a more contemplative people, committing more deeply to prayer as a way of life, and celebrating the liturgy of the Church as an encounter with Christ who sends us out to 'make disciples of all the nations'?

Our Observations

Becoming contemplative means reflecting deeply on

and appreciating the value of authentic living, being aware of the presence of God and living in relationships of love and mutual respect in all aspects of our lives.

An encounter with Jesus means getting to know Jesus in his time and place while appreciating the differences between now and Palestine in 30 AD. Updated liturgies that reflect developments in scripture, theology, anthropology, psychology and historical awareness would engage the imagination and energy of a broader range of Catholics. We need to use inclusive language and modernise the language and forms of liturgy, especially the Eucharist so as to connect directly to the lived experiences of those in the congregations.

We know that in Catholicism, prayer is living the life of Jesus, committing more authentically to life as a way of prayer.

Proposals

That the Plenary Council:

1. Urge parishes and dioceses to provide available and accessible opportunities in every diocese and parish for spiritual growth and development in groups run by lay members of congregations;

2. Encourage the development of meditation, scripture reading groups, groups on being Catholic and other programs to meet local needs and the need for silent listening;

3. Strongly promote the use of inclusive language, and connections to experiences relevant to the congregation in all liturgies;

4. Ensure that every diocese includes in its public annual report a discussion of all these activities and their uptake in parishes.

AGENDA QUESTION 7:

How might we better embrace the diverse liturgical traditions of the Churches which make up the Catholic Church and the cultural gifts of immigrant communities to enrich the spirituality and worship of the Church in Australia?

Our Observations

Ours is a multicultural church in Australia and across the world, and our age is one of multiple forms of identity and expression.

Authentic liturgy emerges from the lived experiences of the participants. People are energised by celebrations that express their faith in forms that are meaningful and reflect value for them.

Different cultures require different expressions. Cultural diversity is not limited to language or ethnicity. Creating opportunities for larger gatherings featuring a coming together of traditions and liturgies will enhance our community experience.

As Pope Francis reminds us, the Eucharist 'is not a prize for the perfect but a powerful medicine and nourishment for the weak'. (Evangelii Gaudium n.47)

There should be no sense of going back or trying to restore practices which are not of today's reality.

We know that many who disengage from the Church do so because they find liturgies dull and uninspiring.

Proposals

That the Plenary Council:

1. Promote liturgical diversity, including varieties of forms of Eucharistic celebrations;

2. Promote and facilitate inter-community and inter-cultural sharing;

3. Promote a welcoming, inclusive culture of Eucharistic sharing for all

who approach the table of the Lord;

4. Commit the Australian Church to advocating for and developing an Australian Rite which expresses our unique circumstances including our heritage of Aboriginal and Torres Strait Islander spirituality, and which acknowledges our history of dispossession, take-over and continuing racism and envisions a future of respect by and for everyone.

Formation

AGENDA QUESTION 8:

How might we better form leaders for mission – adults, children and families, couples and single people?

Our Observations

Baptism is the primary Catholic sacrament. By living it, we become mature Christians. It is time to restore to all Catholics the dignity, authority and responsibilities that have over centuries been taken over by privileged groups in the Church. Catholics must claim their inheritance and take initiative in leading in their communities. It begins by enabling one another to be all that we can be. We need to have strong convictions about our own identities before we can lead others to share our perspectives and values.

The Plenary Council is an opportunity to recognise and implement a synodal process. This is essential for realising the program of Pope Francis. The synodal community is the primary context for the formation of leaders. Ordination is a commissioning to a particularly significant role within the broader context of baptism and community.

This time is an opportunity for further consideration and study of the different 'life-based' methods, and outcomes, of lay formation, including the 'action-reflection' and 'formation through action' models of the Cardijn movements ('See, Judge, Act'), Small Christian Communities, Couple and Family Formation (Teams, Marriage Encounter) and Christian Life Communities. Such small group experiences should start within families and continue through pre-school, at the celebration of the Eucharist and during sacramental preparation, in schools with class retreats and missionary experiences as well as through youth group experiences as part of adolescent formation such as in Antioch.

Leaders emerge and flourish in community contexts, in relation to pressures, demands and opportunities. Mature communities are best placed to recognise and select appropriate leaders. Fostering and developing local communities (parishes) and small groups (intentional communities) in terms of responsibility, freedom and responsiveness to conscience will provide fertile ground for the emergence of leaders in all relevant areas. Leadership requires inclusion, solidarity, synodality, subsidiarity and respect for the sense of faith of the faithful. Vatican II wanted the principle of subsidiarity to permeate all governance, both ecclesial and civil (Declaration on Christian Education, n. 3; Gaudium et Spes Pastoral Constitution on the Church in the Modern World, 1965, n. 8). Ongoing training and understanding of these principles are, for everyone, essential as circumstances, needs and opportunities evolve.

Catholics are often hindered in their understanding and appropriation of our faith by the language in which our theology is presented, especially in liturgies and prayers and the outdated teachings, structures and laws

of our Church. Core doctrines would benefit greatly from being expressed in personalist rather than scholastic or classic philosophical terms. Relevant revisions in these areas would dramatically increase the potential for reaching out to those who have left and those who might wish to join us.

Pastoral Associates do not currently have the autonomy or authority that their roles and responsibilities deserve. Those running sacramental preparation programs are often crippled by outdated theology and overbearing priests. All ministers in the Church are entitled to the freedom of their charisms. Bringing the experiences of women and men, married and single, to the work of enabling our people to reach out to others with good news will yield positive results.

Proposals

That the Plenary Council:

1. Acknowledge that there is a 'lay apostolate' where lay people are co-creators and co-redeemers in the world;

2. Recommend that the bishops establish offices for the laity and adopt a lay pastoral strategy based on the Church's commitment to 'see, judge, act';

3. Ensure that personal and community formation for leadership opportunities are available and accessible in every diocese and parish for all the baptised;

4. Require that all leaders, clerical and lay, embrace qualities of humility, self-awareness, ingenuity, love and heroism and act with accountability, inclusion, safety for all especially children ,and with transparency and in accordance with the

principles of Catholic Social Teaching;

5. Assert that leadership in the Church is based on principles of equality, inclusion, and synodal processes; and that community development and formation programs should reflect this;

6. Require the devolution in every diocese of an appropriate level of authority and autonomy for non-ordained pastoral personnel (especially Pastoral Associates), those managing Sacramental preparation programs (Catechists) and other lay leaders;

7. Strongly support a review of Church teachings that hinder participation by Catholics;

8. Ensure that clergy or lay catechists/pastoral associates reach out to all parents when they present their children for Baptism, Confirmation and Eucharist, and in all situations where effective adult education can take place;

9. Open new pathways to ministry across all ministerial formation for men, women and LGBTIQA+ people which include optional celibacy.

AGENDA QUESTION 9:

How might we better equip ordained ministers to be enablers of missionary discipleship, so that the Church will become more of a 'priestly people' served by the ordained ministry?

Our Observations

All Catholics, cleric and lay, form a priestly people. Optimal equipping and formation of the ordained will come through listening to and understanding our people.

Leadership in the Church is about witnessing and confirming the faith of the people emerging from experience, scripture and tradition and expressed through the consensus of their voices. It is not about defining the faith. The clergy and the hierarchy are ordained to serve the people not to be served by them.

Let our clergy focus on Christian leadership, pastoral care and the spiritual development of a 'priestly people'. Ordained ministers are co-workers with the non-ordained. Working together as equals, women and men will bring enormous benefits to priests as enablers of missionary discipleship and to the whole priestly people.

Both clerics and non-clerics can be involved in Church leadership and, with lay people having more responsible autonomy in administration, assist our priests to work with us on mission. We need to bring the experiences of women and men, married and single, into the work of enabling our people to reach out to others with good news — news that leads to experiences of the Reign of God.

Proposals

That the Plenary Council:

1. Educate ordained ministers and laity to understand that each of us needs to be conscious of, and responsible for, our own spiritual development and means of engaging in the world to bring about the Reign of God;

2. Ensure priests work alongside lay women and men in their roles as pastors and animators, animating the laity to reflect on how to live their lives in the light of the Gospel;

3. Urge ordained ministers to adopt a co-responsible approach with lay Catholics towards the administration and management of parishes to ensure that the ordained ministers and lay Catholics have sufficient time and energy to facilitate missionary discipleship and work towards all Church members becoming more a 'priestly people';

4. Urge dioceses to have a formal formation program for priests coming from overseas that includes local theology, Australian culture, local management practice and style, history, and language and an extended stay with a local priest;

5. Advocate for women and men to lead Sunday reflections/homilies;

6. Urge dioceses to monitor these actions and include them in the public diocesan annual reports;

7. Pursue with the Holy See the ordination of married men to ordained priestly ministry acknowledging that this subject is outside the Canonical brief of the Plenary Council but accepting that this subject is of major concern to those who made Plenary Council submissions;

8. Pursue with the Holy See the ordination of women to the permanent diaconate and priesthood acknowledging that this subject is outside the Canonical brief of the Plenary Council but accepting that this subject is of major concern to those who made Plenary Council submissions.

AGENDA QUESTION 10:

How might formation, both pre- and post-ordination, better foster the development of bishops, priests and deacons as enablers of the universal Christian vocation to holiness lived in missionary discipleship?

Our Observations

The current training of the clergy occurs away from congregations, separated from the world they are being formed to serve, and often without lay teachers, especially women and Aboriginal and Torres Strait Islander people. Priestly formation needs to recognise that the triple grace of priest, prophet and king is bestowed on all the faithful at Baptism, and that the role of the ordained is as fellow travellers and servants of the laity on their journey. Better formation of the ordained will come through listening to and understanding the needs of the faithful they are called to serve.

Deacons, priests and bishops most often do not undertake post-ordination formation, and this must be changed to be in line with all other professions. Such programs should cover a broad range of topics from moral theology, psychology, sociology, administration, leadership and community development to enable them to best understand and serve their congregations. Appropriate lay leaders should assist in developing and teaching these programs.

Proposals

That the Plenary Council:

1. Redevelop formation assessment processes to ensure that candidates for the priesthood are spiritually and psychologically capable of engaging in pastoral care;

2. Redesign priestly training, with students housed in the community and encouraged to engage in the workforce in their long breaks from study, so that they better understand the communities they are being called to serve;

3. Ensure that the teachers of priests in training include women and First Nations people;

4. Include a greater understanding of Christ's call to diversity, with the identification and avoidance of polarisation as core topics in the curriculum;

5. Teach up-to-date management, administration, communication and community development skills as a substantial part of formation;

6. Develop for all ordained ministers mandatory and audited ongoing formation courses including those on management practice and styles;

7. Organise an annual 360-degree performance review for all priests and permanent deacons;

8. Work towards the ordination of women and married men.

Structures

AGENDA QUESTION 11:
How might parishes better become local centres for the formation and animation of missionary disciples?

Our Observations
Personal and community formation are prerequisites for reaching out to others with integrity. With the reduction in clergy numbers and parish amalgamations, existing communities must be recognised and encouraged as centres of faith and support – not as parish outreaches but as the basic communities. The parish is formed through the coming together of these groups. That was the pattern of the early church – from the ground up, not from the top down.

Promote small groups who explore all aspects of Christian living from contemplative prayer to social services to adult Catholic education. When these groups find their motivation in the desires of their members for participation rather than in following directions from 'above', they will flourish, become attractive and grow. They are the primary places of personal and community formation.

Convictions and commitments grow and flourish in a context of personal relationships among people who understand and appreciate one another. When we are valued we become more open to listening to others. We need to be heard ourselves before we can reach out to others.

Parish Pastoral Councils have a key role in this and so need to have appropriate authority and autonomy. Let priests focus on Christian leadership and pastoral and spiritual facilitation.

Within 'parishes' there are usually multiple other Christian churches with whom 'a critical mass of Christian mission' may be possible and fruitful. It may well be that the Church in Australia is being asked to explore ecumenical initiatives within their communities. PPCs should be supported in this.

Proposals
That the Plenary Council:

1. Acknowledge that the traditional concept of 'Parish' needs to take into account that smaller more intimate groups of Catholics are the primary elements of the local parish;

2. Promote small groups/ communities as the primary places of formation and animation for Catholics, recognising their crucial role for the future Church, and empowering them with key decision-making authority;

3. Favour an experiential-based approach to discerning ways forward, e.g., the 'See, Judge, Act' Cardijn or similar action-reflection methods, rather than a 'top down' approach;

4. Require all dioceses to facilitate the creation and development of small group/communities enabling the provision of opportunities for spiritual and personal formation, organised, implemented and managed by lay people;

5. Promote the position that parishes are formed primarily by the coming together of small groups or communities, that each parish is a community of communities and thereby a community for the world;

6. Explore where feasible extending the current interpretation of the 'Catholic parish' to one of an 'ecumenical Christian parish'.

AGENDA QUESTION 12:
How might the Church in Australia be better structured for mission, in consideration of the parish, the diocese, religious orders, the PJPs and new communities?

Our Observations
Structures must ensure the practice of synodality and the principle of subsidiarity whereby decisions are taken by an appropriate entity as close as possible to the people affected by those decisions. In order to develop structures suitable for Australian circumstances, the Australian Catholic Bishops Conference and individual bishops need to introduce changes that respond to local conditions in close consultation with their people.

Baptism is the foundational sacrament through which we become Christians. Ordination is a particular designation of role and function within the community of the baptised. There is no theological reason why pastoral care and governance should necessarily be bound together.

Diocesan pastoral councils, a canonically designated means of involving Christ's faithful in diocesan decision-making, are necessary in all dioceses with functions that include pastoral planning, processes for accountability and transparency in Church activities, and human resource planning, including concerted formation/education plans.

The most effective measures for gaining commitment from people is to involve them in matters that concern them such as participating in decision-making and taking on responsibility for the outcomes of their choices: 'That which touches upon all must be agreed by all'. There is nothing more off-putting to the laity (and people generally) than to be 'consulted' and then disregarded.

Proposals

That the Plenary Council:

1. Accept as fundamental that all decision-making by Church leaders be exercised according to synodality and subsidiarity, thus ensuring accountability, transparency, and inclusion;

2. Ensure that present canonical provisions for structured synodality through diocesan pastoral councils and diocesan synods/assemblies are adopted by all Australian bishops;

3. Require that all pastoral and administrative decisions that affect the faithful must be preceded by consultation with the faithful – 'That which touches upon all must be agreed by all;'

4. Require the establishment of a Diocesan Pastoral Council in every diocese and a Parish Pastoral Council in every parish;

5. Require that a Parish Priest not act against the advice of his Parish Pastoral Council without what is, in his judgement, an overriding reason, and that reason must be noted in the minutes of the Pastoral Council;

6. Require that the functions of Diocesan Pastoral Councils include pastoral planning, concerted education and formation plans including processes for accountability, transparency and human resource management;

7. With reference to the shortage of priests, propose to the Holy See that Canon 517 n. 2 be implemented across Australia so that qualified deacons (men and women), laity (men and women), and religious (men and women) can exercise their 'baptismal priesthood' of providing the true pastoral care needs of a parish; this includes the delegation to baptise, conduct marriages, celebrate funeral services and lead Sunday celebrations in the absence of a priest. (Cf. Roman document of that name issued 1983);

8. Offer opportunities for Christian formation to parents of the young people being catechised for sacraments, taking advantage of the fact that they are present with their children, and advocate for a lay director of pastoral planning in every diocese;

9. Decide membership of Parish Pastoral Councils and Finance Committees by the discernment of all parishioners;

10. Elect members of Diocesan Pastoral Councils are to be elected through a diocesan synod or assembly;

11. Legislate that those matters considered by the ACBC to be outside its competence are to be referred to the competent authority;

12. Require that every diocese in Australia hold a diocesan Assembly at least once every five years;

13. Explore the possibilities social media provide for formation and participation in the future Church, benefiting from our experience during COVID.

Governance

AGENDA QUESTION 13:

How might the People of God, lay and ordained, women and men, approach governance in the spirit of synodality and co-responsibility for more effective proclamation of the Gospel?

Our Observations

People will be drawn to the Church and then to active involvement in Church activities by attraction to what they perceive as an adult, intelligent and responsible attitude to living a worthwhile life. Good governance is an essential element of this attraction. At present, some Australians see the Church as a floundering, inept organisation led by out-of-touch, life-constricted males, or even as corrupt and to be avoided as much as possible.

Proposals

That the Plenary Council:

1. Implement the recommendations of The

Light from the Southern Cross report (cf.5. 'Identification of the Principles and Culture of Good Governance', and 6, 'Good Governance Practices and Culture', pp. 37-115) with a timeline to be audited;

2. Involve and share authority with lay Catholics, openly and in realistic numbers, in the selection of bishops and in the appointment of priests;

3. Adopt the principles of accountability, transparency and inclusion and apply these to all leadership and decision-making in the Church;

4. Ensure full equality for all across all ministries and thus eradicate the culture of clericalism from the Church, in both clergy and laity;

5. Encourage the clergy and hierarchy at parish and diocesan levels, e.g. through adopting Pastoral Councils in all dioceses at parish and diocesan levels, to better recognise the giftedness of the laity while facilitating the proper exercising of their gifts;

6. Enshrine the principles of Catholic social teaching, such as subsidiarity and solidarity, as well as inclusion, equality, transparency and accountability in the mission statements of all parishes, dioceses, DPCs and PPCs.

AGENDA QUESTION 14:
How might we recast governance at every level of the Church in Australia in a more missionary key?

Our Observations

The Church's governance, in structures, culture and practices, must in all respects accord with synodality and the principle of subsidiarity.

Cultural conversion (conversion of the heart) is a huge challenge for humanity as evidenced in many aspects of today's human experience. History tells us that those who currently hold power are less likely to be accepted as successful leaders for such demanding change.

The first challenge is in identifying the change leaders. The second challenge is for the current leadership to accept the need for change and, if possible, get behind the new movement.

The leaders of the new movement will need prayer, broad consultation, discernment and new processes to see the way. Given the Canon Law constraints of the Plenary Council process and its hierarchical leadership, it is likely that the Council will be able to engender only initial steps on this path.

Proposals

That the Plenary Council:

1. Commit to the synodal course directed by Pope Francis as the basis of church governance, processes, and reform;

2. Implement the recommendations of The Light from the Southern Cross report (cf.3, Theological Foundation of the Church, pp. 24-31) with a timeline that can be audited;

3. Recognise the need for deep change and diverse modes of leadership, both clerical and lay;

4. Develop structures which ensure the principles of accountability, transparency and inclusion will be applied to all leadership and decision-making in the Church, and include women in every place where decisions are being made (cf. LSC 5, 6, as for Question 13, Proposal 1);

5. Ensure that the movement for change is based on inclusivity, equality and accountability in eradicating the culture of clericalism from the Church.

Institutions
AGENDA QUESTION 15:
How might we better see the future of Catholic education (primary, secondary and tertiary) through a missionary lens?

Our Observations

Catholic schools are often described as the 'jewel in the crown' of the Catholic Church in Australia. They must offer faith development that takes account of their very diverse communities, and which is closely connected to the real world and at the service of the immediate and future needs of students and their families. Every aspect of school life, not just the Religious Education curriculum, contributes to the students' holistic formation. They are being prepared for a future that, ideally, they will see as a vocation to make visible the Reign of God, whether as Catholics or other well-formed persons, guided by a moral compass inspired and informed by the life and teachings of Jesus, who is the heart of the Catholic school.

All stakeholders in Catholic education need to develop a shared understanding of the theology of mission of the Catholic school. This is so that there are realistic, shared expectations of the role of the Catholic school in the twenty-first century in leading students towards the 'fullness of life' Jesus promised for all who seek to follow his 'Way'.

The teaching of religion needs to be carefully reviewed as part of the Plenary Council's considerations. Twelve years plus of Catholic education currently produces too many young adults who want nothing further to do with the Church and many who simply drift away.

Small group experiences in schools with peer group mentoring continue to receive positive comment by recent graduates. These valuable and important formative experiences have been noted in the formation of adults (see Q 8. above) and manifested for a time with the YCW, Antioch and World Youth Day experiences as examples. These continue to apply as a valid formative pedagogy for young people. In addition, ecumenical approaches to mission amongst young people should also be explored.

It is necessary to examine how religion is taught in schools. This could be done by a detailed survey interviewing teachers, curriculum developers, students (those at school and recently graduated) and parents about their understanding of faith teaching and what they expect from a Catholic education. Schools and teachers, however, cannot be responsible for all the faith development of a young person; for families are also an integral part of this. Social environment influences are also a factor.

If the local church were reflective of the changes expressed above in this paper, youth would have a Church 'home' to transition to as young adults, which they often do not have at present. There is little if anything to attract and 'hold' them in parish or parish involvement.

Proposals

That the Plenary Council:

1. Ensure funding to youth organisations that engage students with both the gospel and life, and produce formed leaders in the church and in society;

2. Review the theological content of religious education curricula to ensure it is a theology for the times, recognising developments in historical awareness, anthropology, sociology, psychology, and medical science, etc.;

3. Strongly encourage teachers of religious education to be formed in theology, spirituality, scriptures and liturgy;

4. Advocate for those in leadership (directors and principals) to view their roles as ministries and have relevant formation offered to them;

5. Urge Catholic schools to set a certain percentage of their enrolments to be offered totally free to families who could otherwise not afford them;

6. Ensure that the school community and families are included in the promotion of parish small groups/communities as the primary places of formation and animation for Catholics.

7. To move from doctrine and apologetics to evangelisation and missionary communities that are relevant to today's issues, and undertake dialogue within these communities in a manner that involves them actively in the real issues of lives and relationships.

AGENDA QUESTION 16:

How might we better see the future of Catholic social services, agencies and health and aged care ministries as key missionary and evangelising agencies?

Our Observations

These services are generally seen by Catholics and others as providers of good and necessary services to all members of the community. For many, they are the face of the Church and should be seen as such, not as appendices. Most of these services have lay leaders and are conducted using principles of accountability, transparency, and inclusion. In some cases there are clerical leaders making autocratic decisions. The leadership of these organisations needs to be transformed to be in line with 21st century best practice.

Pastors could learn much from the experiences of the many disaffected Catholics who continue to work within Church agencies and affiliates. Many have learned to distinguish between being Catholic and engaging with Mass attendance and sacraments.

Proposals

That the Plenary Council:

1. Recognise and support compassionate, sensitive and just engagement with the poor, refugees and asylum seekers, the frail aged, the silenced and those discriminated against in our parishes and beyond as true ministries in the Church;

2. Ensure these services are affordable to those experiencing poverty;

3. Ensure Church leadership continue to support and encourage all forms of Catholic social services, strongly advocating for justice in the public forum;

4. Encourage pastors to be attentive to the voices of disaffected Catholics working in Church agencies and affiliates from whom there is much to be learned.

Conclusion

The Church is an organic entity, a community on the move, an evolving presence of God in the world (one among many). The opportunity provided by the Plenary Council is far broader than the discussions and resolutions possible in two sessions. The Council has the potential to be a catalyst, a fulcrum on which the emerging Church can pivot towards the future. It could be a significant step on the way towards a recovered vision of God's revelation in Jesus and the Spirit within faith communities and in transforming our world and creation.

The immediate challenge for the whole Australian Catholic faith community is to facilitate the work of the Spirit in the Plenary Council in breaking through structural barriers and anachronistic positions to lead us all to a renewed vision of hope and courage.

The extensive participation of the whole People of God in their submissions to the Council was inspirational, reflecting an earnest longing for a revitalised church by Catholics that did not end in 2018-19. Being a synodal Church means involving everyone in ongoing discussions on all aspects of Catholic life. It is about the life and mission of the whole Church community, not just the members and not just the bishops.

We call on Plenary Council members to respond to Pope Francis' hopes for a new era of synodality and accountability where we will all walk together listening to a range of voices. This is the model of Church that Jesus expects from us in this millennium; it will require uncommon courage and a commitment to changes in how we do and are church. For this to happen, we must be open to radical conversion, reform and renewal.

Endorsed by the Australasian Catholic Coalition for Church Reform (ACCCR) and its members

Australian Reforming Catholics

Be the Change Aotearoa (NZ)

Cardijn Community Australia

Catholics For Renewal

Catholics Speak Out

Communities of the Way (WA)

Concerned Catholics Canberra Goulburn

Concerned Catholics Tasmania

Concerned Catholics Wagga Wagga

Concerned Catholics Wollongong

Cyber Christian Community (WA)

For the Innocents

Inclusive Catholics

Rainbow Catholics InterAgency for Ministry

SA Catholics for an Evolving Church

Toowoomba Catholics for Church Reform

VOCAL (Voices of Catholic Australian Laity)

WATAC (Women and the Australian Church)

WWITCH (Women's Wisdom in the Church)

ACCCR Co-conveners: Eleanor Flynn (dremflynn@gmail.com) and Peter Johnstone (pjgovernance@gmail.com)

For discussion:

1. Noting the key themes of 'THE AUSTRALIAN PLENARY COUNCIL: An Agenda for Reform?' listed in the Executive Summary, are there other themes that you would stress?

2. What priorities and concrete proposals would you suggest to Plenary Council members to ensure a successful Plenary Council?

3. How can the Plenary Council best 'respond to Pope Francis' hopes for a new era of synodality and accountability where we all walk humbly together'?

4. Let's all pray together that the Holy Spirit will guide Plenary Council members in their task of ensuring that the Council is 'a catalyst, a fulcrum on which the emerging Church can pivot towards the future'.

Endnotes

1. Eliot, T S, *The Complete Poems and Plays of T.S Eliot: Four Quartets*, Little Gidding, p 197, Faber and Faber, London, 1969.

2. Hunt, M E, *Fierce Tenderness: A Feminist Theology of Friendship*, p. 13, Crossroads, New York, 1994.

3. Carroll, J, *Toward a New Catholic Church: The Promise of Reform*, p. 15, New York: Mariner Books, 2002.

4. Carroll, J, *Toward a New Catholic Church: The Promise of Reform*, p. 15, New York: Mariner Books, 2002.

5. Hunt, M E, *Fierce Tenderness: A Feminist Theology of Friendship*, p. 41, Crossroads, New York, 1994.

6. Williams, R, 'Christianity: Public Religion and the Common Good', lecture given in St Andrew's Cathedral, Singapore, 12 May; accessed at https://aoc2013.brix. fatbeehive.com/articles.php/1165/ christianity-public-religion-and-the-common-good

7. Women of WIT, 'This is My Body: On Violence and Vulnerability in Women's Experiences', posted November 23, 2010. https://womenintheology. org/2010/11/23/this-is-my-body-on-violence-and-vulnerability-in-women%e2%80%99s-experience/

8. Women of WIT, 'This is My Body: On Violence and Vulnerability in Women's Experiences', posted November 23, 2010 https://womenintheology. org/2010/11/23/this-is-my-body-on-violence-and-vulnerability-in-women%e2%80%99s-experience/

9. White Ribbon Australia Website, 'Understanding the Issue', https://www.whiteribbon.org. au/Primary-Preventatives/ Understanding-The-Cause

10. Morley, J, *All Desires Known*, p. 27, SPCK, America, 1994.

11. *America Magazine*, February 26, 2019.

12. Comensoli, P, The Way of the Gospel: Families of Communities, Address to Archdiocesan Clergy, Bulleen, Victoria, April 28 2021.

13. Vatican II wanted the principle of subsidiarity to permeate all governance, both ecclesial and civil: Declaration on Christian Education, n. 3; *Gaudium et Spes* (Pastoral Constitution on the Church in the Modern World), 1965, n. 86.

14. Canons 511-514

15. Grech, M, General Secretary for the Synod of Bishops, Vatican News, 21 May 2021, accessed 18 July 2021 at https://www. vaticannews.va/en/vatican-city/ news/2021-05/cardinal-grech-interview-synod-secretariat-changes.html

16. Grech, M, ibid.

17. Canon 127, §2.

garratt PUBLISHING

Published in Australia by Garratt Publishing 32 Glenvale Crescent Mulgrave VIC 3170 www.garrattpublishing.com.au

Cover & Text Design by Guy Holt Edited by Greg Hill Cover image iStock All photographs © iStock except for pages 28 & 31 © Alamy (Geraldine Doogue quote on back cover: https://www.eurekastreet.com. au/article/why-i-m-still-a-catholic) (Prof Hans Zollner SJ quote on back cover: https://therecord.com.au/news/ local/exclusive-vatican-expert-gives-insight-into-abuse-crises/)

Printed by Advent Printing

ISBN 9781922484239

NATIONAL LIBRARY OF AUSTRALIA — A catalogue record for this book is available from the National Library of Australia

Cataloguing in Publication information for this title is available from the National Library of Australia. www.nla.gov.au

The authors and publisher gratefully acknowledge the permission granted to reproduce the copyright material in this book. Every effort has been made to trace copyright holders and to obtain their permission for the use of copyright material.

The publisher apologises for any errors or omissions in the above list and would be grateful if notified of any corrections that should be incorporated in future reprints or editions of this book.

Further reading on the Australian Plenary from Garratt Publishing

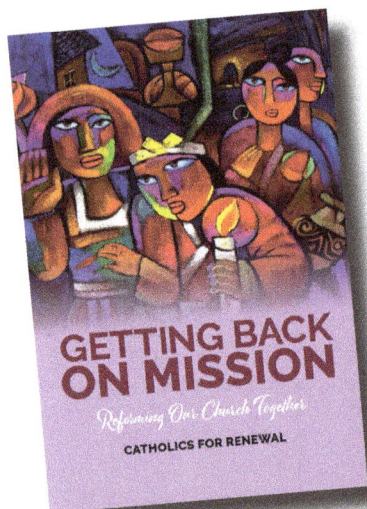

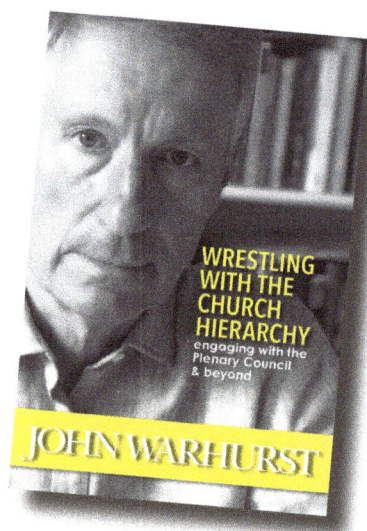

Getting Back on Mission

The Catholic Church has gone 'off mission'. The scandal and tragedies of clerical child sexual abuse and the cover-up by bishops is symptomatic of a deeply ailing church. Getting Back on Mission focuses on Jesus' mission for the Church; it exposes dysfunctional governance involving a grave lack of accountability and transparency, and the exclusion of the People of God – particularly women.

This is a contribution to the Australian Plenary Council 2020/21. Its purpose is twofold: to get the Church back 'on mission'; and to show how that can be achieved 'together'. The reforms proposed are based on sound evidence and analysis. For Catholics wanting genuine renewal of their Church, this roadmap for change is a must-read and an essential companion book for the Plenary Council.

Getting Back on Mission is forward-looking and founded on trust in the Spirit – it is about hope.

Catholics for Renewal is a group of committed Catholics that has been advocating Church renewal for a decade. A legion of Catholics has supported its work involving surveys, open letters, articles, and public evidence at major government inquiries. Catholics for Renewal believes that the Church will change only if individual Catholics take up the challenge and drive that change – and many renewal groups throughout Australia are doing just that.

Catholics for Renewal is a member of the Australasian Catholic Coalition for Church Reform.

'... a realistic, hopeful and authentically Catholic roadmap for the forthcoming Australian Plenary Council...'
– Frank Brennan SJ, AO

'I hope this book helps navigate our Church's sacred pastors to the wisdom and action needed to get us out of this mess.'
– Mary McAleese, former President of Ireland

Wrestling with the Church Hierarchy: Engaging with the Plenary Council & Beyond

John Warhurst's unique perspective as a Church insider-outsider means that he walks a fine line. As an insider, he works within the Church in many leadership and governance roles; as an outsider, he leads ginger groups and lobbies for change through both Church and mainstream media.

Wrestling with the Church Hierarchy is a personal account of attempting to come to grips with the power structure of the Church at a time of necessary reform of those structures. As a forceful but understanding critic, John shows no fear or favour when dealing with Church authorities. He is adamant that the Church needs many more women in leadership positions, greater lay participation in co-responsible governance, and much more extensive transparency and accountability in all aspects of Church affairs, including finance and communications.

John considers the Plenary Council 2021-2022 a crucial once-in-a-generation opportunity to advance these reforms. But it's not the only opportunity. John's message is that the time for dioceses and parishes to introduce reforms is now.

John Warhurst AO is Emeritus Professor of Political Science at the Australian National University, Chair of Concerned Catholics Canberra Goulburn (a member of the Australasian Catholic Coalition for Church Reform) and a Delegate to the Plenary Council. He was co-author of The Light from the Southern Cross: Promoting Co-responsible Governance in the Catholic Church in Australia.

For sales enquiries:
W: www.garrattpublishing.com.au
E: sales@garrattpublishing.com.au
T: 1300 650 878

www.ingramcontent.com/pod-product-compliance
Lightning Source LLC
Chambersburg PA
CBHW061021090426
42742CB00025B/3473